THE LEADERSHIP BOOK OF NUMBERS
(VOLUME 2)

Short Tips for the Leader on the Go to Help You Grow the Business, Develop Your Professional Life, and Lead Others More Effectively

Navigating Your Course toward Greater Effectiveness in…
SERVICE EXCELLENCE • LEADERSHIP • HR/LEARNING & DEVELOPMENT

By
THEO GILBERT-JAMISON

AuthorHouse™
1663 Liberty Drive
Bloomington, IN 47403
www.authorhouse.com
Phone: 1-800-839-8640

© 2012 Theo Gilbert-Jamison. All rights reserved.

www.psbydesign.com

No part of this book may be reproduced, stored in a retrieval system, or transmitted by any means without the written permission of the author.

Published by AuthorHouse 7/9/2012

ISBN: 978-1-4772-0892-2 (e)
ISBN: 978-1-4772-0893-9 (hc)
ISBN: 978-1-4772-0894-6 (sc)

Library of Congress Control Number: 2008900663

Any people depicted in stock imagery provided by Thinkstock are models, and such images are being used for illustrative purposes only.
Certain stock imagery © Thinkstock.

This book is printed on acid-free paper.

Because of the dynamic nature of the Internet, any web addresses or links contained in this book may have changed since publication and may no longer be valid. The views expressed in this work are solely those of the author and do not necessarily reflect the views of the publisher, and the publisher hereby disclaims any responsibility for them.

Introduction

This book is a continuum of Volume I of *The Leadership Book of Numbers*. The purpose of this book is to provide emerging, high potential, and aspiring leaders with simple tips to increase their effectiveness, lead their teams, and create and sustain a culture of excellence.

Just as with Volume I, this book is intended to be an easy read. Something you can take on your next business trip and complete within three to four days. We intentionally titled this series, The Book of Numbers, because most of my readers like information that is broken down into short lists and tips that they can use to enhance their effectiveness.

I have divided this book into three sections: Service Excellence, Leadership, and Human Resource/Learning & Development. Each section is written to include clever tips to enhance your daily walk as a leader. As in all of my writings, I have repeated key insights a number of times from one chapter to another. This is intentional to get your attention and to move you to action.

To get the most out of this book, read it from cover-to-cover or pick out and read in any order those chapters that deal with your immediate issues. Highlight information that inspires you. Then commit to applying something you have learned, and sharing it with others.

I wish you every success in your pursuit of service, performance, and operational excellence and would like to start you off with one of my favorite quotes from Mahatma Gandhi…

> *"The journey of a thousand miles begins with one step."*

TABLE OF CONTENTS

PART 1 - SERVICE EXCELLENCE

Chapter 1	Creating & Sustaining Service Excellence	3
Chapter 2	The Role of Senior Leadership in Driving Excellence	7
Chapter 3	The Role of Mid-Managers in Driving Excellence	10
Chapter 4	Creating a Memorable Customer Experience – The 5 Steps	14
Chapter 5	Five Reasons Employees are Cynical about Vision & Mission	17
Chapter 6	Six Things A Leader Should Never Assume	21
Chapter 7	Providing Service Excellence to Internal Customers	26
Chapter 8	Taking the Mystery Out of Mystery Shopping – The 5 Essentials	30
Chapter 9	Creating Employee Engagement – The 5 Key Elements	33

PART 2 - LEADERSHIP EFFECTIVENESS

Chapter 10	The Seven Signs of a Bad Boss	39
Chapter 11	Ten Critical Expectations of Leadership	43
Chapter 12	Leadership through Accountability – The 5 Essentials	46
Chapter 13	Enhancing Business Acumen – The 5 Key Elements	50
Chapter 14	Developing Powerful Presentation Skills	53
Chapter 15	The Power of Professional Presence – The 20 Basics	59
Chapter 16	Confronting Unacceptable Behavior – The 8 Essentials	63
Chapter 17	Delegation, Empowerment, and Time Management – The 5 Essentials	67
Chapter 18	Interviewing with Excellence – The 10 Essentials	71
Chapter 19	Driving Results with a Lean Staff – The 15 Essentials	76

| Chapter 20 | Overcoming Tough Economic Times – The Ten Imperatives | 80 |
| Chapter 21 | Top 5 Mistakes Managers Make in Recessionary Times | 85 |

PART 3 - HUMAN RESOURCE, EMPLOYEE LEARNING & DEVELOPMENT

Chapter 22	Fifteen Standards Every HR Department Should Live By	91
Chapter 23	Gaining the Support of Your C-Level – The 5 Essentials	94
Chapter 24	The Top Ten Ways to Recruit and Retain Highly Talented Employees	97
Chapter 25	Creating Training that Sticks – The Top 10 Tips	103
Chapter 26	Getting the Most Out of Web-based Training	106
Chapter 27	Employee Training & Development during Lean Times – The 5 Essentials	110

Conclusion	113
Acknowledgement	114
About the Author	115
Other Books by Theo Gilbert-Jamison	116
Index	117

PART 1
SERVICE EXCELLENCE

Chapter 1

Creating & Sustaining Service Excellence

Occasionally I am fortunate to work with model companies, who truly value my expertise and follow *(to the letter)* the roadmap laid out for them, with tremendous success. This inspired me to share my Top 10 Musts for Ensuring Success in Creating and Sustaining a Culture of Service Excellence. As we go through these essentials, I urge you to identify which ones you should be focused on to strengthen your brand promise.

1. **Senior Leadership MUST be actively involved**. When the CEO and other C-Level Executives are involved in the process from start to finish, it demonstrates the importance and value of service excellence within the organization. Standing on the sideline, periodically cheering the team on is not enough. I have worked with organizations great and small across all industries, and those where the CEO or highest ranking executive were part of the process experienced the greatest levels of sustainable success, employee buy-in, and return on investment.

2. **Service Excellence MUST be a company-wide initiative**. Every department must be responsible for delivering an exceptional customer experience, whether they deal primarily with external or internal customers. When service excellence training is relegated to just one area or only to front-line staff, employee enthusiasm and buy-in are short lived. Employees, especially those at the front-line, must see and feel that everyone within the organization is supporting them in driving excellence from the boardroom to the storeroom.

3. **There MUST be employee involvement throughout the process.** When employees are involved in the planning of work that affects them, their level of support and buy-in are immeasurable. No one wants a customer service initiative shoved down their throat without their input and feedback being taken into consideration. Employees who are part of the solution help champion the cause, are more apt to hold themselves and their peers accountable for driving excellence, and have a greater sense of pride and fulfillment in their work.

4. **A Project Owner MUST be established.** The responsibility of getting teams together, scheduling follow-up meetings and training sessions, and ensuring information gets communicated system-wide must be delegated. The Project Owner's role should be perceived as one of distinction, honor, and empowerment; not just extra work. The CEO should hand select the right person. Someone who is liked and well-respected among their peers; has great communication skills *(verbal and written)*; and possesses excellent organizational skills. Most of all, the role must be delegated to someone who truly wants it.

5. **Customer Service Expectations MUST be established.** What are the key touch points that make up an exceptional customer experience? The answers cannot be left to chance. You cannot assume that all leaders and staff are aligned with what an exceptional customer experience should *look, feel,* and *sound* like. It must be established, regularly reinforced, and measured. This should also be outlined in your organization or team's standards of excellence, often referred to as Service Standards.

6. **Customer Service Expectations MUST be integrated into every aspect of the work environment.** How do I accomplish this, you might ask? Well the answer is simple, through on-going employee learning and development; performance reviews that measure the employee's ability to bring the organization's vision, mission, and values to life; reward and recognition of sustained superior performance; and of course, on-

going communication. Most likely you already have the right tools and resources at your disposal, just make sure you are properly using them to reinforce excellence.

7. **Departmental and Team Leaders MUST be held accountable.** We always make it clear to supervisors and mid-level managers that the success or failure of any service excellence endeavor lies within their hands. If they are committed, walk-the-talk, and foster a work environment that makes it easy for their team to drive excellence – the initiative will result in long-term success. If they are negative, cynical, or skeptical, the initiative will slowly fade and become just another unsuccessful program of the month. Leaders must clearly understand their role in driving excellence, and be held accountable to it.

8. **Monthly targets MUST be set.** What gets measured, rewarded, and recognized, gets done! When monthly targets are set it is easier to identify and celebrate accomplishments. At the beginning of the service excellence endeavor, monthly *(or even quarterly)* goals and expectations should be established and communicated, with routine follow-up to ensure that goals and expectations remain the focus of the initiative.

9. **Communication updates MUST be regular and consistent.** Every form of communication used within the organization should be resourced to ensure a consistent message is delivered. Employee newsletters, the company intranet, internal blogs, and senior leadership communication should all be aligned when it comes to reinforcing and fostering a culture of service excellence. Communication cannot be hit or miss, it should be monthly at a minimum. Sporadically sharing updates every couple of months is ineffective.

10. **Everyone throughout the organization MUST remain vigilant.** Even when it looks and feels like nothing is changing, change may very well be occurring. And because change takes time, especially in larger

organizations, everyone must remain vigilant and optimistic. Most important, when it looks like the organization is getting off track, senior leadership must step up to ensure everyone stays focused on driving excellence.

Bottom-line, these top ten musts are not all-inclusive. However, my hope is that it inspires you to search out ways to ensure service excellence is a sustainable focus within your organization.

Summary Questions

- Which of the top 10 musts are weaknesses within your organization?

- Which are strengths?

- What can you do to impact service excellence within your organization?

Chapter 2

The Role of Senior Leadership in Driving Excellence

Creating a culture of service, performance, and operational excellence is a journey, not a destination. And guess what? As soon as you feel you have achieved it, along comes increased competition which forces you to be more innovative in your approach.

Unfortunately, without commitment, strong leadership, role modeling, and innovation, it is impossible to maintain a competitive advantage within any industry. So, *what is the role of senior leadership in driving excellence? And, why is their involvement central to the achievement and sustainability of service, performance, and operational excellence?*

SENIOR LEADERSHIP'S ROLE

1. **Set the Vision.** In driving excellence, senior leadership is responsible for setting the vision of the organization. They must provide clarity concerning where the organization is going, and what it aspires to be in 5, 10, or 15 years. The vision should be clear and simple; an inspirational message that engages stakeholders at all levels, from the storeroom to the boardroom. Maybe your vision is for the organization to be a global leader in your industry, or to be a valued contributor within the community. Whatever it is, it must move from your head to the hearts and minds of your employees.

2. **Be a Champion of Excellence**. Senior Leadership cannot relegate driving excellence to someone else, because they are too busy to be

bothered with it. They must be the #1 guardian of excellence within the organization. This means talking about it regularly, and demonstrating it in their daily interactions with customers and employees. If they don't have time to champion the cause, it sends the wrong message to your employees.

3. **Communicate What You Expect.** Senior Leadership must use every opportunity available *(employee meetings, newsletters, videos, electronic media)* to share from their perspective how driving a higher level of excellence will not only impact the organization's financial bottom-line, but how it will increase business and revenue, which creates greater opportunities for growth and advancement for all employees.

4. **Create a WE mentality.** Senior Leadership must create an environment that is all-inclusive in driving excellence. They should use words like "WE" and "OUR" as often as possible when communicating. This verbalizes that senior leadership is part of the initiative, and not just standing on the sidelines refereeing and waiting to penalize employees who screw up.

5. **Involve Employees.** Senior Leadership must engage line staff in the process of driving excellence by soliciting their input, acting on ideas and solutions that will advance the organization, and by recognizing sustained, superior performance. Employees who are encouraged to be involved in the planning of work that affects them are more apt to support the initiative wholeheartedly, and foster a spirit of buy-in within their team.

6. **Hold Mid-Managers Accountable**. Senior Leadership must make it clear to all mid-managers and supervisors, that compromise in driving excellence is not an option; and that they are relying on everyone's active involvement throughout the process. They must use internal tools and resources to measure what is expected *(i.e., productivity or quality reports,*

performance reviews, and incentive plans). Mid-managers who achieve or exceed expectations in driving excellence should be readily rewarded and recognized. While those who fall below expectations should be coached and counseled to ensure improved performance.

So, why is senior leadership involvement central to the achievement and sustainability of service, performance, and operational excellence? Because in the organization's journey to drive excellence, every move they make will be closely scrutinized. Their actions and behaviors will set the tone and determine the achievement and sustainability of the organization's vision, mission, and values.

Bottom-line, when senior leaders incorporate these six essentials as part of their regime in driving excellence, they can leave the rest up to their mid-managers and supervisors. But, senior leaders must never forget that driving excellence starts with them.

In the end, they will demonstrate clearly with their *words, actions,* and *behaviors* that they are seriously committed when it comes to creating a culture of service, performance, and operational excellence.

SUMMARY QUESTIONS

- *Is your senior leadership actively involved in creating and sustaining a culture of service excellence?*

- *Which of the six essentials do they put the most emphasis on?*

- *What can you do to impact service excellence within your organization?*

Chapter 3

The Role of Mid-Managers in Driving Excellence

Mid-managers and supervisors also play a significant role in creating and sustaining a culture of service, performance, and operational excellence. In Chapter 2, I shared six essentials in the role of senior leadership *(consisting of your CEO, CFO, COO, and even the CLO)*. Now allow me to elaborate further and clarify the role of mid-management and supervisors in driving excellence.

Why is the mid-manager's role so crucial?

Mid-managers and supervisors have direct impact on both the work environment created for their line staff, and the overall customer experience. However, too often mid-managers and supervisors are not held to any level of accountability when it comes to employee performance and customer service. The focus is solely on operations.

The Mid-Manager's Role

1. **Align with the Vision & Mission.** As mentioned previously, creating a clear organizational vision, mission, and business objectives that every employee can rally behind is the responsibility of senior leadership. Subsequently, the role of mid-management is to align their team to ensure all job activities, job priorities, and overall contributions are consistent with the organization's vision and mission. In order to align your team, you must be familiar with the vision, mission, and business

objectives; clearly understand how they relate to your business unit; and have a sound strategy to meet or exceed them.

2. **Set Service Expectations.** In driving excellence, employees need a clear understanding of what excellence should *look, sound,* and *feel* like. Your role as a leader is to develop departmental expectations that will ensure consistency in service delivery. Service expectations should cover what a customer should experience from start to finish; including all of the key touch points that make up the customer experience. This should be done for every department.

3. **Integrate Expectations into the Work Environment.** Once the expectations are established, they should be integrated into the performance review process, be part of job specific training, used to recognize exemplary job performance, and as a coaching tool when improvement is required. First and foremost, these expectations should be reviewed when interviewing new job candidates to ensure they have a clear idea of what is expected from the onset.

4. **Communicate Often.** When it comes to creating a culture of service, performance, and operational excellence – repetition is good. Just as it takes twenty-one times *(of consistently doing something)* to form a habit, mid-managers need to talk about the vision, mission, and business objectives with their team regularly so it becomes second-nature. Share stories, simple work examples, and best practices that demonstrate how other teams drive excellence to make it real and relevant for your team. The more you talk about the vision, mission, and business objectives – the more familiar your team will become with them.

5. **Hold Team Accountable for Excellence.** Let everyone know that you will be holding them accountable for consistently driving excellence. Once you have established the service expectations, continue to communicate them, and ask employees for examples of how they

contribute to bringing them to life in their daily work. When an employee falls below performance expectations in their job, take immediate action by jumping into your coaching and counseling mode. Don't be afraid to confront unacceptable behavior of employees that may be stifling the team's ability to drive excellence.

6. **Reward and Recognize Superior Performance.** When an employee consistently exceeds the established service expectations, openly reward and recognize them. Make a big deal of it by genuinely showing them that you appreciate their efforts. Something as simple as a pat on the back, a certificate of appreciation, or even a handwritten note cost almost nothing.

Bottom-line, if you incorporate these six essentials as part of your regime in driving excellence, you will be on the road to creating sustainable change within the work environment. Never forget that the responsibility of driving excellence includes you. So, take a moment and assess your current level of engagement and commitment to driving excellence, then identify what you must START, STOP, or CONTINUE doing and implement a timeline by which you will act on your commitments.

In the end, you will demonstrate clearly with your *words*, *actions*, and *behaviors* that you are seriously committed to creating a culture of service, performance, and operational excellence. And most importantly, senior leadership will perceive you as a valued contributor to the success of the organization.

> **SUMMARY QUESTIONS**
>
> - *Which essentials are you regularly demonstrating in driving excellence?*
>
> - *Which do you need to work on?*
>
> - *What is standing in the way in of fulfilling your role in driving excellence?*

Chapter 4

Creating a Memorable Customer Experience – The 5 Steps

All customers deserve a premium experience. They have spent hard earned money with your establishment, so why would you want to rob them of this?

In browsing through a trade magazine I came across an ad for a product that guarantees they will deliver a great customer experience. Why aren't more companies delivering on this promise? It really doesn't take much strategy to accomplish it. There are the five simple steps to deliver a great customer experience:

1. **Find out what your customer likes.** *What do they consider an exceptional experience?* This cannot be done by sitting around the boardroom table with your staff and brainstorming or assuming what a great experience might feel like. To truly deliver on a great experience, you must ask your customers. We achieve this through impromptu interviews, focus groups, surveys, or one-on-one conversations. By just asking we get closest to identifying what a great experience looks and feels like for them.

2. **Determine the cost of non-compliance.** *What would it cost to deliver a great customer experience?* You may need to invest in new technology, a facility upgrade or renovation, additional staff, or additional training. *Is it worth it?* When I pinpoint precisely what the customer wants from their perspective, it usually cost less than I anticipated. And, I almost always receive a quick return on investment through repeat business and increased sales.

What will it cost your company if you do <u>not</u> invest in creating a great customer experience? If it will cost you loyal customers who leave and choose a competitor who provides these enhanced services and products, then the cost of non-compliance might be more than you can afford to risk.

3. **Re-evaluate your service or product.** *When was the last time you actually purchased or used your product? Does it really stand up to your customer promise?* If you always get your company's products or services for free, you will never have the same appreciation or lack thereof as a paying customer. When I worked for a luxury hotel company, I traveled around the world at their expense. Naturally, every experience was impeccable from my perspective. However, after I left the company and vacationed at one of these same luxury hotels at my own expense, my perspective was different. I was somewhat disappointed because the experience did not live up to the price. I no longer had on rose colored glasses. Now I looked at every interaction from a paying customer's perspective.

   Consider this, *if you had to pay for your company's product or service, would you be extremely satisfied with it?* If the answer is *"no"* or you are not sure, I can guarantee your customer is not *consistently* receiving a great experience. Fix it!

4. **Ensure you have the team to deliver a great customer experience.** *Do you have a core team of highly talented, exemplary employees who can deliver on the promise?* If the answer is *"no"*, don't waste financial resources on renovations and technology upgrades before you invest in getting the right people on the team. In the final analysis what the customer appreciates most and finds valuable is the human interaction. Bottom-line, you cannot deliver a great customer experience without having the right people on your team. Let me reiterate, it cannot be done. If it means you must rebuild your team, do so gradually until you get what you need to accomplish the goal.

5. **Strategize to deliver a great customer experience.** *What is your strategy to ensure the experience is consistent?* If there is no strategy, the experience will be ad hoc at best. Without a strategy, you will only create pockets of excellence; and overall, pockets of excellence do not equate to a sustainable, great customer experience.

At a minimum, there must be a 30-60-90 day strategy with realistic timelines, and action steps assigned to specific team members. To ensure sustainability, the strategy should extend to a 12-24 month action plan that is in writing and reviewed at quarterly intervals, with strong team accountability for achieving results. Great customer experiences do not happen by chance. It is a process that is well thought out from start to finish. If you want to create a premium brand, built on an impeccable product or service, there must be a plan or strategy to ensure you stay on task.

Bottom line, 90% of senior leaders, mid-managers, and staff members know exactly what is necessary to drive excellence and create an exceptional customer experience. Sadly, only 10% act on it because for the majority it is easier to procrastinate or ignore the issue at hand. If you really want to create great customer experiences start with these five simple steps. Undoubtedly they will help you strengthen your brand, increase customer loyalty and ultimately impact bottom-line results.

SUMMARY QUESTIONS

- *Has your organization defined what a memorable customer experience should look, sound, and feel like?*

- *Is it acted on by employees at all levels?*

- *What can you do to enlighten your team so they provide a higher level of service?*

Chapter 5

Five Reasons Employees are Cynical about Vision & Mission

I spend a lot of time on the road sharing the concepts of my first book *The Six Principles of Service Excellence*. A few years back, I was fortunate to travel the U.S. with Vistage International and speak specifically to CEOs and business owners across all industries. This experience gave me great insight into the hearts and minds of individuals who spend a great deal of their time working to strengthen the profit potential, growth, and effectiveness of their brands.

I found that many CEOs were highly enthusiastic and driven by their organizational vision and mission. However, there were some who were somewhat reticent about vision and mission statements as a whole, and tended to think that their employees felt the same way. Therefore, they invested no time clarifying what their organization could be through the vision and mission.

There's no doubt that most of these CEOs run relatively successful organizations; the question is *"how much more successful and effective could their organization be if they invested time and thought to clarifying the vision, mission, and business objectives for their employees?"* During these trips a CEO once said, *"My employees are cynical about the vision and mission"*. I replied with the five reasons why.

1. **They are not involved in its creation, but largely accountable for executing it.** Too often senior executives sequester themselves to the boardroom for hours, drafting the company vision and mission

statements. At the end of this exhaustive effort they are extremely pleased with the document and can't wait to share it with the field. Within a few days it is distributed to all leaders with a directive to review it with staff and *make it happen*. This is absolutely the wrong approach to gaining employee buy-in and support. The manager is given no direction or support and left to his or her own devices to engage employees around the document.

A more effective approach is to select a team of exemplary employees consisting of senior leaders, mid-managers, and a few front-line, support and administrative workers to draft the vision, mission and core values of the organization. Next, it should be reviewed with senior leadership for approval and refinement; then distribute the refined draft to all employees throughout the organization for review and feedback.

After everyone has been given ample opportunity to provide their suggestions and opinions of the drafted documents, it should be again refined, adopted, and reviewed with all staff. This way, when the manager is directed to share the new vision, mission and core values or service standards with their team, it will be a familiar document that was created based on everyone's input.

2. **The vision and mission statements are too long.** Some vision and mission statements are simply too wordy. If your vision statement is more than one sentence, most likely it will not be memorable to employees. A vision statement is a short sentence with the purpose of articulating what the organization aspires to be within 5, 10, or 15 years; it clarifies the organization's future or desired state. If your mission statement is more than 3 sentences, it is also too long. A mission statement is comprised of a few short sentences that clarify and summarize what the organization is about, its purpose or legacy, why it exists.

Great vision and mission statements are simple, clear, and easy to memorize. If yours does not meet the criteria, do something about it! Select a small team of exemplary employees to refine or rewrite it. Most employees and managers that we meet detest long, complicated vision and mission statements; especially if they are required to memorize them.

3. **The vision and mission don't make sense to them.** When vision and mission statements are filled with a lot of complicated terms, to staff it sounds like *mumbo-jumbo* that doesn't make sense. Long vision and mission statements that are written by senior executives without any input from mid-management and front line employees can be confusing to everyone, even the people writing them. And certainly, if something doesn't make sense to employees, how on earth can they bring it to life?

Remember, complexity often fosters confusion and misalignment, while simplicity often creates clarity and alignment. The more simplified your vision and mission statements, the easier it will be for all stakeholders to embrace; and it will certainly become a tool with which you can hold everyone accountable for driving excellence.

4. **The vision and mission are written as marketing tools to attract customers.** When vision and mission statements are written solely as marketing tools it can be dangerous because the intent behind the message is wrong. I have seen this done on several occasions and poorly executed. Vision and mission statements should be written as timeless documents that provide employees with direction, guidance and clarity about the organization.

Once you are able to create a work environment where the vision and mission are truly energized every day, then it's time to consider using it as a marketing tool. To do so beforehand is like putting the cart before the horse.

5. **No one makes time to explain it to them.** The same amount of enthusiasm, vigor and diligence that are dedicated to creating or refining your vision or mission statements should be committed to devising a strategy for communicating it to all employees. When these documents are shoved into employee's faces without much explanation, it fuels cynicism. Every opportunity that senior leadership has to discuss the vision and mission of the company should be taken advantage of; using common examples of how to bring the vision and mission to life that all staff can connect with and embrace.

Opportunities to explain the vision and mission can arise during new *employee orientation, departmental meetings, or at employee general sessions*; also in simple language, written in the employee newsletter, or in an email tagline. Be creative and enthusiastic about explaining the vision and mission, and employees will be inspired to energize it every day.

Hopefully you have identified a few areas where you can improve. Bringing the vision and mission to life starts with you, using an inside-out approach. Start with yourself and eventually others will want to follow your lead.

SUMMARY QUESTIONS

- *How do employees feel about your organization's vision and mission?*

- *How do your senior leaders feel about it?*

- *How can you help change the perception from cynicism to optimism?*

Chapter 6

Six Things A Leader Should Never Assume

In my twenty years of experience as a Hotel Executive, then as a Performance Consultant and Executive Coach, I have come to realize that in too many circumstances leaders assume way too much.

As with most Performance Consultants, before entering any initiative with an organization, I always seek to learn as much as possible about the organization. I am particularly interested in finding out what the organization stands for, what is its' core, what is its' purpose. Some clients find this intrusive, and some cannot clearly answer these questions. Only a few really get it.

Naturally, most senior executives are well-versed on the inner workings of their organization. Eloquently, they can articulate the vision, mission, and purpose of the organization. With ease and clarity they can also rattle off the organization's business objectives, what excellence should look like to their customers, and how to appropriately handle customer problems that might occur. However, the problem I find is that this clear cut understanding of the organization does not trickle down to frontline staff.

Giving senior leaders the benefit of the doubt, I ask, *"if I walked into your office today, stopped the first employee I encountered, and ask them to tell me what the objectives or key priorities of the company are, what would I hear?"* At the senior leadership level they are often confident that their employees will make them proud. They have no doubt that employees will answer my question in the same manner that they have. *"Why not? We talk about this all the time,"* is the typical response I get. However, this is rarely the case when meeting with employees.

For the most part, leadership assumptions about what employees know and feel are incorrect. Most employees are clueless because leaders do a poor job of bringing the core values, service philosophy and key priorities of the organization to life for employees. To close this gap in leadership effectiveness, there are six things no leader should assume.

1. *Never assume employees understand their* **PURPOSE**.
2. *Never assume employees connect with the* **VISION & MISSION**.
3. *Never assume employees connect with the* **BUSINESS OBJECTIVES**.
4. *Never assume employees know what is necessary to achieve* **EXCELLENCE**.
5. *Never assume employees know how to properly* **RESOLVE** *customer problems*.
6. *Never assume employees will* **TIRE** *of hearing your message*.

PURPOSE - When new employees begin work with an organization they are excited and enthusiastic about their future; they look forward to contributing to the company's success. However, within a few weeks that feeling of being part of something exceptional fades if they do not clearly understand the purpose of their work. At the very core, the purpose of most jobs *(especially those in the service industry)* is to create a high-quality product, a memorable customer experience, or maybe an exceptional work environment where excellence can thrive. When employees understand this, they too have a greater opportunity to thrive. When employees are not aware of their *purpose*, they tend to focus only on the functional aspects of the job which leads to a very routine, bland existence and eventually an inconsistent, substandard customer experience. When employees understand their *purpose*, the customer experience is enhanced; it is delightful, and especially memorable.

In brands like Starbucks, Chic-fila, Nordstrom, Lexus, and The Ritz-Carlton employee purpose is demonstrated in consistent, superior levels of service. Of course, these organizations are industry benchmarks when it comes to helping employees understand and connect with purpose because they *never assume employees understand their purpose*.

Vision & Mission - As a leader it is your responsibility to ensure that every employee within your circle of influence understands the vision and mission of your team and the organization as a whole. A vision statement verbalizes the desired or future aspirations of a team or organization. A mission statement clarifies the purpose of a team or organization, it reaffirms the legacy you want to leave.

What does your organization stand for? Is it integrity, honesty, trust, teamwork, respect, or quality? Your role as a leader is to make the vision and mission clear and plain; to be an example of how it is brought to life through your actions and behaviors; and to hold employees accountable for energizing it every day through mentoring, role modeling, and staff development.

Employees will not connect with the vision or mission if you do not talk about it regularly. Your job is to help them understand how it correlates with their everyday work and the level of service they are expected to deliver. *Never assume employees connect with the vision and mission.*

Business Objectives - *What are the goals, objectives, and key priorities of your organization?* Is it higher profits, increased customer satisfaction or loyalty, waste reduction, higher employee morale and productivity, growth and expansion? Whatever they are, every employee should be apprised of them. Every organization should have 3-5 key priorities that are quantifiable, and that simplistically communicate what is needed to excel. As stated earlier, senior executives have a clear perspective on what is necessary to drive excellence, but that information rarely trickles down to the administrative, support, operations, and frontline staff. As a result, the key priorities of the organization get lost in the monotony of daily tasks and are rarely achieved. *Never assume employees understand the business objectives and how their work contributes to achieving them.*

Excellence - *What does a flawless service experience look like or consist of?* It could be happy customers, served by friendly and attentive staff, who deliver a quality product in a good work environment. Whatever it is for your team or organization, your employees will not get this visual through ESP. You must tell them, then show them through your consistent actions and behaviors. Experience has proven that when excellence is not clearly defined and reinforced by leadership, it results in the delivery of inconsistent service or pockets of excellence, at best. *Never assume employees know what is necessary to achieve excellence.*

PROBLEM RESOLUTION - Most employees do a lousy job of customer service recovery because there is no methodology or process in place to ensure success. Therefore, employees are left to their own devices to figure out the best way to fix a problem. This generally leads to a win-lose situation for either the customer or your organization. To create the win-win, teach your employees the five steps to effective problem resolution, then reward and recognize those who consistently do it well. The five steps are: (1) **Listen** *to the problem*; (2) **Empathize** *with the customer*; (3) **Ask** *how you can resolve the problem*; (4) **Produce** *a realistic solution*; then (5) **Follow-up** *to ensure the customer is satisfied with the resolution.*

Not providing proper training and coaching, or role playing on how to handle routine customer issues is a surefire route to disaster and customers dissatisfaction. Constantly communicate, clarify and reinforce the five step problem resolution process and you will gradually create a work environment where employee empowerment can thrive. When employees feel confident and competent to resolve routine departmental and customer issues, it frees you up to focus on taking the team to the next level. *Never assume employees know how to properly resolve customer problems.*

COMMUNICATION - It takes twenty-one days of repetition to form a habit. The same philosophy applies to your leadership message or mantra. If you are passionate about service excellence or delivering a high quality product, you must talk about it on a consistent basis *(at least 21 times)* in order for it to become second nature and engrained in the hearts and minds of your team. What you dedicate most of your time and communication to, is what employees will remember most.

Your message concerning the vision, mission, core values, standards of service, and business objectives must be consistent, simple, and delivered with enthusiasm, and vigor. You must never tire of bringing these themes to life for your team. This is your moral obligation as a leader of others. Just as employees feel they never get enough pay or reward and recognition for their work, they also feel there is never enough open-communication concerning important issues within the organization. *Never assume employees will tire of hearing your message of service excellence.*

So what are your next steps? Now that I've got your mind racing, certainly there are a multitude of other things you have surfaced that a manager should never assume. Others are: *Never assume veteran employees don't need retraining; Never assume you spend enough time recognizing the exemplary work of employees; Never assume your communication is clear to everyone.* I could go on and on. I encourage you to start with the six false assumptions outlined in this chapter, and create a plan of action to close those gaps.

SUMMARY QUESTIONS

- *What are some of the false assumptions your leaders have about the organizational vision and mission?*

- *How are these false assumptions impacting the work environment?*

- *What can you do to close the gap on these false assumptions?*

Chapter 7

Providing Service Excellence to Internal Customers

Many leaders assume that when they refer to internal customers in casual conversation or in training sessions with employees, that everyone is on the same page and knows exactly what they are talking about. But the reality is that many employees have no concept of what an internal customer is, or why it is important to consider how they are treated in driving excellence.

So for the purposes of alignment, the business definition of *an internal customer is someone within your organization who relies on you for a particular product or service to get their job done.* An internal customer could be a fellow co-worker, colleague, another department or business unit; and in some instances it could even be a supplier or vendor that has a strong partnership with your organization.

On the other hand, external customer is a term that most employees are more familiar with – because they are defined as someone who pays money for your company's products or services.

Why is focusing on the internal customer so important? Most customer service experts would agree that *"if you are not serving the customer, your job most likely is to be serving someone who is!"* It is also true that when internal customers feel a sense of value and contribution to organizational success, they in-turn are more motivated to provide exceptional customer service to everyone they encounter – albeit their fellow co-workers or paying customers.

In addition, when internal customers feel valued and respected in the workplace they:

- *Are less likely to make mistakes that impact others, and more eager and willing to correct errors should they occur*

- *Are more willing to work synergistically with other departments in the spirit of teamwork and collaboration*

- *Want to see the organization succeed, and therefore work efficiently and productively to do their part*

- *Demonstrate a sense of urgency and self-accountability in getting their work done*

Enhancing internal customer service has a trickle-down effect, and leadership *(top-down)* sets the tone. Simply put, in order for service excellence to thrive, everyone must consistently emulate actions and behaviors that demonstrate a unified commitment to excellence in the treatment of internal, as well as external customers. Examples of how co-workers bring this to life are:

1. Always greet colleagues, co-workers, and team members with a warm and friendly smile.
2. Commit to learning something unique about your fellow team members *(their likes and dislikes)* to provide a higher level of service.
3. Based on their likes and dislikes, always try to anticipate the needs of co-workers so that you personalize the service experience or product provided to them.
4. As a sign of respect, commit to learning the names of your co-workers, using them as much as possible.
5. When interacting with co-workers, use positive eye contact to indicate that you are interested and attentive to their needs.
6. When conversing with others, always listen carefully and empathically with your ears, eyes, and heart.
7. Be polite in your speech with each other, using words like *"I'll be happy to," "please,"* and *"thank you."*

8. Use proper telephone etiquette, even when answering the call of a co-worker. Answer all calls with a smile, thanking the caller, giving them your name, using hold carefully, and keeping them updated if they are on hold – regardless of whether it is an external or internal customer, a manager or a subordinate.
9. If a co-worker or colleague has experienced a problem with your work, don't take it personally, apologize and work to resolve it quickly. Then follow-up to ensure their satisfaction.
10. Your personal appearance and work area are not only reflections of you, but also of your entire team. Always maintain a professional appearance and a clean, organized work area.
11. If a fellow employee appears to be lost or needs directions, take a moment to escort them to their destination -- instead of pointing our directions.

Again, these are standards of excellence that should be consistently exemplified whether you are dealing with the CEO of your organization or Susie the mailroom clerk. In providing service excellence to internal customers, every employee is treated with the highest levels of dignity and respect.

I know you may be saying to yourself, *"this stuff sounds easy, but no one treats me like this."* Well, the power of one person making a difference is cataclysmic, and you my friend can make a tremendous difference within your organization. However, in order to do so you must commit to being a role model in driving internal and external customer service and be passionate about it by staying optimistic; sharing with others why it is important, surrounding yourself with like-minded colleagues; and staying consistent.

A great guiding principle to remember is that *we are all service professionals who serve someone.* Even if you never see a customer, most likely you provide a service to someone who does. Therefore, we all contribute to creating a memorable service experience, for both our internal and external customers.

SUMMARY QUESTIONS

- *Do your employees know what an internal customer is?*

- *Are internal customers within your organization treated with the same level of dignity and respect as external customers?*

- *What can you do to ensure your staff also provides service excellence to their internal customers?*

Chapter 8

Taking the Mystery Out of Mystery Shopping – The 5 Essentials

Mystery Shops are a great way to assess and reinforce exceptional service experiences. However, most employees have a negative perception of Mystery Shoppers. They consider it an unnecessary tool that intimidates and is used only to spotlight service deficiencies, never highlighting the good.

The true purpose of Mystery Shoppers are to help businesses positively impact sales by increasing employee awareness of the level of service they are providing. When done effectively, business owners who use these services get a more realistic picture of how their customers perceive their company.

Mystery Shop Reports are a good measure for banks, hotels, retail stores, and restaurants, but don't limit them to those industries only. They can also be extremely beneficial for law firms, healthcare organizations, manufacturing plants, or even consulting firms. The sky is the limit. To ensure your Mystery Shop process is a win-win for all concerned, here are five essentials to remember:

1. **Key Touch Points** – establish the five to ten key touch points that should happen with every customer interaction. Examples of key touch points might be: *Customer is immediately greeted or acknowledged upon entering our store; Employee introduces themself, then asks for the customer's name, and how they might be of assistance; Employees carefully listens to customer, gives positive eye contact, smiles and uses customer's name throughout the interaction; Employees are knowledgeable of products they are showing the customer; If there is a problem, employees offers realistic*

options; *The transaction is accurately processed; Customer is thanked, asked to come again, and escorted to the door.* A big mistake we often make is not outlining what the Mystery Shopper should be listening and looking for.

2. **Checklist** – Create a detailed checklist to ensure key touch points, that are important to the service experience are not overlooked. Ensure the key touch points on the checklist are quantifiable, measured on a five or ten point scale, so it is not subjective. This will also give you comparative data from month to month or quarter to quarter. Most professional Mystery Shop companies have some form of assessment or checklist they use. Your job is to tailor it to meet your specific needs.

3. **Mystery Shopper Selection** – Select your Mystery Shoppers wisely. Choose people who understand your business, corporate culture, and brand. Choose people who possess great attention to detail, those who have a good idea of how an exceptional service experience or product should look or feel. A big mistake we make is selecting friends, family members, or others who don't know what to look for.

4. **Employee Training & Follow Up** – Ensure your employees understand why you conduct mystery shops. What is its purpose? Make sure they are aware of the process, the checklist of things the shopper will be looking for, and what happens to the mystery shop report. Then use the tool *(mystery shop report)* to determine training needs, as well as individual coaching needed for employees who are not meeting performance expectations. Be sure to reward and recognize employees who constantly go above and beyond in creating an exceptional service experience, especially those employees whose names are consistently mentioned in the shopper's reports in a positive light.

5. **Measurement** – Create a simple, visually interesting scorecard that shows progress over time, and post it in locations that are visible to

all employees. A good scorecard will show both positive and negative trends by business unit and department, if possible. Post good comments alongside photos of those employees who consistently excel during mystery shops.

Remember, the purpose of Mystery Shoppers are to help businesses increase sales and improve employee awareness of the level of service they are providing. Yes, they should remain impromptu and unexpected events for the employee. However, it should also be a positive learning experience that enhances employee performance and promotes positive morale. If your employees do not have a good perception of the process, then you have some work to do. By starting with these five simple steps, we guarantee the process will be more productive and positively welcomed by all concerned.

SUMMARY QUESTIONS

- *Do you use a Mystery Shop process or something similar to assess service?*

- *Do your employees perceive it positively or negatively?*

- *How could you use this type process to impact the level of service your team delivers?*

Chapter 9

Creating Employee Engagement – The 5 Key Elements

In creating a culture of service, performance, and operational excellence, employee engagement is the key that unlocks the door to customer loyalty. Unfortunately, the leadership skills needed to create an environment that fosters employee engagement, motivation, and trust are often elusive in many organizations.

During my travels and interactions with thousands of line employees *(in varied industries)*, I kept hearing five common things that they *want*, *need*, and *expect* from leaders to be more productive, valuable, and promotable within the organization.

1. **Communication** - When polled *(across all industries)* few employees felt that they had received enough communication or information on company updates from their boss. Open communication is key to creating and sustaining a culture of excellence, as well as, increasing employee engagement and trust, customer loyalty, and ultimately improving bottom-line results.

   Open communication can be in the form of: *one-on-one* updates with staff members; daily briefings with the entire team; company newsletters and intranet updates; or through regularly scheduled team or departmental meetings.

   Open communication does not mean sharing confidential company information, but it should include keeping your staff abreast of intercompany changes, financial results, customer feedback *(good or bad)*, and aware of new products and services that will soon be launched.

Remember, from the employee's perspective, there is always something new to share, and when you open the lines of communication, you lessen the likelihood of negative gossip.

2. **INVOLVEMENT** - Creating fully engaged employees, who have passion for driving excellence, also includes involvement. Most employees we polled *want to be involved* in the planning of work that affects them. When employees are not involved it often contributes to misalignment, negativity, and low morale.

Involving employees doesn't mean getting their say on confidential business issues, but it does include soliciting their feedback on workplace issues, processes or procedural changes that will impact their work -- before they are implemented. When employees understand the *"why"* and are involved to some extent in the improvement process and implementation, you have a greater chance at creating sustainable change, a high level of trust, buy-in, and support.

3. **TOOLS & RESOURCES** - When employees are provided with the proper equipment, tools and resources to do a quality job, it creates a great environment for holding everyone accountable for driving excellence. It also demonstrates that the organization is serious about creating a work environment where employees can thrive, be successful, and contribute to improving operational and financial results.

Basic tools and resources should include appropriate supplies and equipment, along with learning and development opportunities to enhance employee competence, confidence, skill, and ability.

When was the last time you assessed where you stand (as a leader) in providing the basic tools and resources to ensure a job well done from your staff? If funding and budget cuts are barriers, I suggest you use the wisdom of your team to surface resourceful ways to ensure they have what they need, while not causing a financial burden to the organization.

4. **RECOGNITION** - Even in organizations who profess that they do a good job in rewarding and recognizing staff members, there are still many employees starving for it. That's because the level of recognition initiated often varies based on the departmental leader. I believe that there should be multiple channels of reward and recognition flowing throughout an organization, not only top-down recognition – which is manager-to-employee, but also unilateral recognition – which is peer-to-peer.

When employees feel they are adequately recognized for a *job well done*, they become self-motivated to do *more with less*. And for the most part, a sincere *"thank you"* with a pat on the back from a manager or senior leader to a line employee can go a long way in creating and sustaining a culture of excellence.

5. **TRUST** - When leaders work diligently to keep the lines of communication open, involve employees in the planning of work that impacts them, provide employees with proper tools and resources, and consistently recognize exemplary job performance – all of these elements contribute to creating a high level of trust on both sides of the fence.

Bottom-line, there are other elements that contribute to employee engagement, and each organization's work environment is different. However, it all starts with leaders knowing what their employees want and expect, and being firmly committed to creating an environment where workers are engaged and committed to driving excellence.

SUMMARY QUESTIONS

- *What do you believe are key elements in getting your employees fully engaged?*

- *What are you doing to meet employee expectations?*

- *How does employee engagement impact the level of service your customers receive?*

Part 2
Leadership Effectiveness

Chapter 10

The Seven Signs of a Bad Boss

It's tough enough to be working in a sometimes unstable environment with the threat of job losses and cost-cutting measures. However, top it off with working for a Bad Boss, and you may very well have a recipe for professional disaster. Studies verify that each year, Bad Bosses negatively impact the work environment by fostering high levels of employee frustration, stress, resentment, and eventually high labor turnover throughout the company.

There are seven signs of a Bad Boss. As you review them, take a few minutes to assess both your effectiveness and ineffectiveness as a leader. *Honestly, how often do you fall prey to these seven signs?*

1. **Bad Bosses Have No Clear Goals.** If your team has no clue of the goals or expectations they should be working towards, this may be a weak area for you. We find in such cases, that there are either no goals at all; the goals are unrealistic; or they are unclear to the team. This leads your team to assume that either their boss doesn't know what they are doing, doesn't care, or doesn't want them to be in the loop.

2. **Bad Bosses Deliver Poor or No Communication.** These are the silent types, who revel in their team not knowing what they are thinking. Bad Bosses don't feel it necessary to communicate how the company is doing, nor how employees are performing in their jobs. They just don't communicate, and rarely show any emotion – good or bad.

3. **Bad Bosses Hold No One Accountable.** When there is no communication of team standards or goals, Bad Bosses really can't hold

anyone accountable for excellence or even mediocre job performance. Bad Bosses are apt to turn a blind eye, allowing rampant compromise throughout the workplace – and in spite of their lack of accountability, they are not approachable and some employees even fear them.

4. **Bad Bosses Often Blame Others.** When things don't go as they planned or expected, they are quick to point fingers at everyone except themselves – especially when their team doesn't perform up to standard. While self-accountability is out of the question, Bad Bosses find it easy to blame inefficient work systems, processes, and staff members *(all within their sphere of control)* for their inability to meet company-wide goals and performance standards.

5. **Bad Bosses Have No Strategy for Improvement or Team Success.** Stubbornly believing that strategizing is a waste of time, they just don't bother with it. Bad Bosses have a false belief that they are doing fine as is; and because often the powers that be *(senior leaders and board members)* don't hold them accountable for positive change, things remain in a constant state of confusion for both customers and employees.

6. **Bad Bosses Never Delegate.** To mask their fear of employee empowerment, Bad Bosses fail to properly train and delegate challenging tasks to their team members. They are very cynical when it comes to their team, and don't feel that anyone has the intellect or capacity to perform their job satisfactorily. Therefore, the team remains stagnant and virtually paralyzed in the absence of leadership.

7. **Bad Bosses Don't Mentor Others.** From their perspective training, staff development, and mentoring are also a waste of time. They often say, "No one ever mentored or developed me and I turned out alright." Bad Bosses have no concept of how to synergistically collaborate with their team to help them grow and excel in their jobs. Unfortunately, they practice *"tough love"* when it comes to on-the-job training.

In assessing and changing bad behaviors, take a minute and evaluate your current workplace. *How many of these poor leadership behaviors do you or your leaders regularly exhibit? When you are treated like this, how does it make you feel?* If this information has helped you surface some of your blind spots, now is a good time to make a change and to increase your effectiveness as a leader.

If you have identified more than three poor leadership qualities that you regularly exhibit *(for your team's sake)* it's time to make a change. Here are a few simple suggestions to help you improve:

- *Find a mentor or an executive coach, someone you would consider a trusted advisor and seek their help in making incremental behavioral changes*

- *Commit to learning all you can about your primary leadership style, blind spots, and how to overcome them*

- *Create a personal/professional action plan with realistic timelines by which you are committed to changing*

- *Eventually, apologize to your staff, let them know that you are committed to change and begin becoming the person you want them to emulate*

While Bad Bosses negatively impact the work environment by fostering high levels of employee frustration, stress, resentment, and unnecessary labor turnover – there are simple things that every leader can do to improve the work environment and drive excellence. *It just takes a little commitment!*

SUMMARY QUESTIONS

- *Have you ever worked for a boss who regularly demonstrated these poor leadership qualities?*

- *How did it make you feel?*

- *What can you do to ensure you don't fall prey to these poor leadership behaviors?*

Chapter 11

Ten Critical Expectations of Leadership

In order for leaders to perform at optimal levels, just like line staff, they must have a clear understanding of what is expected of them. It is senior leadership's responsibility to identify the expectations and standards of performance for their leadership body. Doing so clarifies those universal actions and behaviors that are expected from every leader (top-down) to achieve excellence, enhance the work environment, and impact bottom-line results. Most important, it increases morale by creating leadership self-accountability for success.

If you have leadership *service or performance standards*, this list is a great benchmark to determine its strength and effectiveness. If not, it is a great place to begin building leadership commitment and accountability for driving excellence.

1. **Service Philosophy** - *We are committed to our company's service philosophy. We are responsible for being a living example of it every day, and removing any barriers that prevent our employees from energizing it every day.*

2. **Business Goals** - *We support and encourage the achievement of our company's business goals. We hold ourselves and our team accountable for contributing to and achieving positive results.*

3. **Innovation** - *We foster an environment of innovation and continuous improvement. By supporting positive change, we work to increase the productivity, effectiveness, and long-term success of our business units.*

4. **ETHICS** – We demonstrate the highest levels of integrity and ethics in our business dealings. We protect the confidentiality of proprietary company information, as well as employee information. We operate our business unit with the highest regard to legal and government (federal, state, and local) regulatory compliance standards.

5. **RESPONSIVENESS** – We provide instant pacification to our employees (when possible) and follow through on their ideas, suggestions and/or concerns. Any leader who receives a question, inquiry or complaint owns it and will follow through to completion within 24 hours.

6. **RELATIONSHIPS** - We treat our customers and every employee with the highest degree of dignity, respect, and professionalism. We are responsible for creating an atmosphere of teamwork and positivity for all employees, promoting the Open Door Policy whenever possible. We reward and recognize exemplary performance that contributes to organizational success.

7. **EXECUTION** – We properly allocate our time and resources to ensure the key priorities of the organization are achieved. We effectively delegate both routine and important tasks and decisions, develop and use systems to track and disseminate organizational information. We make decisions in a timely manner to ensure worker productivity and remain centered on meeting key business objectives.

8. **TALENT DEVELOPMENT** – We ensure all employees are properly trained in their job within their first 30-days of work, providing coaching and feedback as needed to optimize job performance. We proactively identify and develop talent within our organization by regularly providing learning and development opportunities that foster career growth and advancement. We give timely and specific feedback to employees and discuss problems immediately, before they are forgotten or get out of control.

9. **COMMUNICATION** – We regularly share relevant information to help others understand and support business objectives, empathically listening

and responding to their needs to foster positive two-way communication. We are responsible for holding department meetings (quarterly at a minimum) to keep the team aligned and updated on company issues, performance expectations, and other pertinent information.

10. **EMPOWERMENT** – *We identify the root causes of our chronic issues, seek ways to resolve them, then properly train our employees so they are competent, confident, and empowered to resolve issues should they arise. We are responsible for training our employees on the basics of problem resolution and empowerment to ensure alignment, consistency, and customer satisfaction.*

Hopefully this list has provided you with some inspiration and direction. These leadership standards or expectations can also be used to evaluate and measure leadership effectiveness and performance. Bottom-line, don't leave your leaders in the dark concerning performance expectations. Give them a clear-cut understanding of what is expected and the resources to achieve them, and you will see measurable results.

SUMMARY QUESTIONS

- *What are some of the expectations your organization has established for its leaders?*

- *How do they impact your job performance?*

- *How do they impact the overall work environment?*

Chapter 12

Leadership through Accountability – The 5 Essentials

So many workplace issues, from employee job performance and engagement, to driving business results, customer loyalty, and profitability could be easily resolved if more managers engaged in holding themselves and their team accountable.

Accountability for some seems to be a bad word that leads to low worker morale. Some see it as a form of workplace bullying, but there is nothing further from the truth. I once met a leader who would proudly proclaim that she was a very *"hands off"* manager, especially when her division head questioned her inability to effectively lead her team. Based on the constant low performance of her team, it was evident that she had a hard time holding her staff accountable.

The word *accountability* is often inaccurately defined, and ineffectively used. In the workplace, accountability is defined as the act of holding others responsible or answerable for their actions *(good or bad)*, for exemplary job performance, and achieving business results.

Accountability is not demoralizing staff members for the sake of making a point or an example of them. It is not directing staff members in a condescending manner, or by fear and intimidation. Accountability is about setting the expectation, clearly communicating it, and then holding yourself and everyone within your sphere of influence responsible for consistently meeting the established expectations.

Accountability is a process, with a beginning and an end. It is not about telling people what you expect them to do, then quickly moving on to the next thing.

As I travel the country sharing *The Six Principles of Service Excellence*, I espouse the importance of leadership and employee accountability in creating a sustaining culture of service excellence. While many leaders strongly agree, few know what is necessary to ensure accountability in the workplace.

There are five specific steps to holding employees accountable for excellence. Growing up a young manager in The Ritz-Carlton organization, senior leaders used these five steps with such a high level of intensity, genuiness, and finesse that we had no option but to accept personal accountability for driving excellence.

1. **Clearly define the expectation or standard.** *People cannot be held accountable for what they have not been informed of.* Don't assume employees know what a good job looks like. Paint the picture by clarifying, detailing, and outlining what you expect. Keep in mind, you don't clarify expectations after something goes wrong, at that point you should be reinforcing them. Here's an example of what I'm speaking of: Excellence in an office setting, at the reception desk, means the workplace is immaculate, spotless; telephone calls are answered within three rings *(and with a smile)*; employees are appropriately attired, wearing their proper name tag; every visitor who enters the reception area is immediately welcomed with a warm and friendly greeting, and the receptionist uses their name when and if possible.

2. **Involve staff in efforts to raise the bar.** Once the expectations have been defined, they should be shared with employees during staff meetings. Then staff members should be given an opportunity to voice their opinions or concerns regarding the new standard. To ensure clarity and gain buy-in, ask questions like: *Do you think that we can achieve this new standard? What do you believe might stand in the way? What potential*

barriers might we face? What do we need (i.e. tools, resources, training) to consistently meet the new standard or expectation? In the long run, giving employees an opportunity to voice their concerns will enhance their commitment and support of the new standard or expectation. It demonstrates that you care, value their opinions, and that you are committed to making them a part of the solution -- not just forcing the new standard down their throats.

3. **Integrate the new standard.** Now it's time for all of the talking, team brainstorming, and sharing of ideas and best practices to turn into action. To definitively build accountability, the newly agreed upon standard or expectation must be fully integrated into every aspect of the work environment – to include the training and development process, performance review criteria, and all applicable systems and work processes. This shows that you are thorough, mean business, and have a sustainability strategy in mind. *And guess what?* Your team should be 100% involved in this process -- again to build teamwork, camaraderie, and to make them feel like valued contributors to the organization's success.

4. **Set measurements to quantify success.** Use internal key indicators or measurements to assess how effective the team is in following and upholding the new standard or expectation. Key indicators might include *customer satisfaction survey results, employee satisfaction survey results, productivity reports,* or even *labor turnover results.* If your company doesn't have a process in place to measure key indicators like these, then work with your team to create a simplistic scorecard that everyone can understand and support.

5. **Recognize success, and coach for improved performance.** Make it a priority to regularly acknowledge and reward employees who consistently exemplify the new standard or expectation. This not only encourages them to keep up the good work, but it also sets the standard by which

everyone should be measured. And don't overlook those employees who fall below the standard by not consistently meeting performance expectations. Commit to routine coaching and counseling, working with them on an improvement plan to help them achieve success.

Bottom-line, effective accountability involves a process. It is not just directing employees on what to do and then going on about your business. Your success as a leader is contingent upon your ability to achieve business results through people, and that cannot be achieved without holding everyone accountable for driving excellence.

SUMMARY QUESTIONS

- *Do you feel you do a good job of holding employees accountable for driving excellence?*

- *Which of the five steps do you need to improve on?*

- *How will improving in this area help you create and sustain a culture of service, performance, and operational excellence?*

Chapter 13

Enhancing Business Acumen – The 5 Key Elements

In order to run an effective, dynamic, and successful organization, leaders must possess sound business acumen. Unfortunately, we are not born with this vital leadership skill, it is cultivated over time. When asked to define business acumen, the response of senior leadership is basic and straight forward. Most believe that business acumen means having financial savvy; but that is only one element of business acumen.

There are five essential components that make up sound business acumen: *Intelligence, Strategy, Communication, Innovation,* and *Accountability*. As you review the qualities of each, assess yourself as well as other leaders on your team to see where strengths and weaknesses exist within your organization. Then start on an action plan to close those identified gaps and elevate organizational success to the next level.

1. **Intelligence:** Yes, leaders possessing this component of business acumen are skilled at creating, reading, and analyzing financial reports and budgets. However, they are also at ease when it comes to explaining this sometimes complex information to others. This is a quality that most senior leaders admire and think of when they envision someone with great business acumen. Along with financial savvy, leaders possessing this component of business acumen have an insatiable hunger to learn more and increase their knowledge and intellect. They not only read business books, magazines and white papers to gain knowledge, but also

to glean skills and techniques that can be applied in their line of business and daily work.

2. **STRATEGY:** Leaders possessing this component of business acumen know the key priorities *(goals and objectives)* of the organization, and have proactively formulated a written action plan to get the team there. They don't wait for the strategic plan to come down the pike from headquarters; as soon as they get wind of the key business objectives they begin focusing on how their team will contribute to and impact it. Again, having business intelligence is not enough, leaders must also be able to turn all that wealth of knowledge into actionable behaviors that will engage an entire workforce or team and drive positive results.

3. **COMMUNICATION:** Leaders possessing this component of business acumen are excellent communicators, both verbally and in writing. They know that simple, clear communication is the key to achievement of the key business priorities and strategy. If you ever observe leaders with great communication skills, you will notice that they communicate clearly up and down the organizational ladder. They can get a point across with finesse at the executive level, and simplify the message with ease to relate it to the day-to-day activities of line staff.

4. **INNOVATION & RESOURCEFULNESS:** Leaders possessing this component of business acumen have the keen ability to work with little, and produce much. They are not limited by a lack of resources, but innovative enough to create new ways of getting the job done effectively and efficiently. While having all of the tools at their disposal to do the job properly would be great, they do not allow the lack thereof to create team dissention or negativity. Their greatest joy comes from being able to overcome barriers and obstacles to create a product or service that is exceptionally better than they ever expected. Leaders who possess sound business acumen are not wasteful, but innovative and resourceful.

5. **ACCOUNTABILITY:** Leaders possessing this final component of business acumen understand the importance of employee accountability in optimizing productivity to achieve success. Without accountability none of the other components that make up sound business acumen *(intelligence, strategy, communication and innovation)* will be of any worth. In order to hold employees accountable for driving the key priorities of the organization the leader must set the standard or expectation, communicate it to enlist employee buy-in, integrate it into every aspect of the work environment, evaluate employee performance against it, then reward and recognize those who consistently meet and exceed the expectation or standard.

Just like a waterfall, business acumen starts at the top *(with leadership)* and trickles down throughout the entire workforce. If leadership does not possess these essential components, organizational effectiveness and success are not sustainable.

Now that you've been equipped with some level of clarity concerning business acumen, the next step is to work toward closing your professional gaps. Bottom-line, developing sound business acumen does not start or stop with becoming skilled at analyzing financial reports. Developing sound business acumen is multi-dimensional.

SUMMARY QUESTIONS

- *Which of the five components of business acumen are your strengths?*
- *Which components do you need to improve?*
- *How will enhancing business acumen make you a better leader?*

Chapter 14

Developing Powerful Presentation Skills

Whether you are sharing new information with the board of directors to gain approval, or with your team to gain support and buy-in for a new initiative, effective presentation skills are paramount. That's because effective or powerful presentations are not just about relaying information in the form of *facts* and *figures*, but oftentimes it also enlists positive persuasion skills to gain commitment.

To increase your effectiveness in getting our point across with a high level of audience attention, retention, and engagement there are three essentials: **Preparation, Presentation,** and **Feedback for Refinement.**

#1 Preparation *(Before the Meeting)*

- **Know your audience.** The first key to delivering a powerful presentation that enlists positive results is to prepare in advance. This starts with knowing your audience – *their likes, dislikes, expectations, and hot buttons.* In my experience I've found that some audiences enjoy humor to add levity to the presentation, while other audiences just want the pure facts and figures.

- **Know your topic.** Preparation also means knowing your topic inside and outside; anticipating the types of questions the audience might ask; and being able to answer them in a quick and concise manner. If you are not committed to becoming a *"subject matter expert"* on the topic you are asked to discuss, don't commit to the assignment. The last thing you want is to be perceived as a babbling idiot in front of your superiors and colleagues. Again, you MUST know your stuff, inside and out.

- **Outline your presentation**. Even the most powerful public speakers will admit that they outline their presentation in advance. This ensures they stay on point and cover those issues that are most important to the audience. It's easy to get side-tracked by questions from audience members that are not relevant to your topic or message. Having a thorough, brief outline helps you get back on track and ensures the audience leaves with the message you intended them to have.

- **Have Handouts**. It is rare that you get the allotted time promised to present your information. Most meetings, especially at the executive level always run over time – which sometimes limits the amount of time you have to present your topic or message. Having brief handouts that outline or reinforce the most important points of your message are always helpful. Also, be mindful that the quality of your handouts speak volumes to the audience about your level of expertise, and your attention to detail. For those members of the audience who are very visual, this also adds value and clarity on the topic and message you want to deliver. If your PowerPoint presentation is short, 5-10 slides, you can make it the handout.

- **Practice makes perfect.** As a subject matter expert, I give speeches, presentations, and facilitate training workshops on the topics related to *Service Excellence* and *Leadership Effectiveness* several times a month -- and have written several books on these topics. However, I still rehearse my presentation in private *(aloud)* several times, reviewing my notes leading up to the minute of my presentation to ensure success. Just like you, I have only one chance to make a *first impression*, and not being prepared by practicing in advance is a perfect formula to destroy that first impression.

- **Walk the room in advance.** If possible, always gain access to the training or meeting room in advance to give you an idea of the set-up. Then check your equipment and software *(i.e., LCD projector, laptop computer, PowerPoint presentation, microphone, wireless mouse)* in advance to ensure there will be no technology or equipment issues before you start. The last thing you want people to remember about your presentation is that the equipment didn't work. Another part of the preparation process is knowing your topic or presentation so well that if there is an equipment issue or malfunction you are still able to deliver the information or message with a high degree of confidence. Bottom-line, always be prepared. Never assume the equipment will function without incident.

- **Dress appropriately.** It should go without saying, *but I will mention it* – appearance is very important, no matter who you are presenting to. Looking your best gives the positive impression that you are prepared, knowledgeable of your topic, confident and successful. Even if the attire for the audience is casual, dress one level up – which would be *"business casual."*

#2 **PRESENTATION** (*Your Delivery during the Meeting*)

- **It's OK to be nervous.** Again, the best way to overcome nervousness is to *be prepared* and *know your topic* better than anyone else. Eventually your nervousness will subside.

- **Speak clearly and with confidence.** Pace yourself, so as not to speak too fast or too slow – because both drive audiences crazy. If you have difficulty enunciating certain words, do not use them. Also, be careful not to speak in a monotone manner; it will put people to sleep.

- **Be mindful of your body language.** A genuine smile is a great way to warm a group up, so be very conscientious of your facial expressions throughout your presentation. Your body language should be relaxed to convey confidence, and throughout your presentation be sure to scan the room with positive eye contact and a periodic smile. If your eyes focus solely on your presentation notes or the PowerPoint slides on the projection screen throughout the entire presentation you will lose the audience, and not be able to determine whether they are embracing the message or are bored stiff. Also, be extremely mindful of your posture and hand gestures. Remember; not only is the audience *listening* to you – they are also *looking* at you.

- **Make your presentation memorable**. Start with a strong opening, typically interesting facts and figures are a good way to get the audience stirred, or with a little taste of humor. Next, make sure you have an impactful middle -- this is where your knowledge and expertise of the subject will make all of the difference. Don't lose the audience with too many big words, but at the same time don't talk down to the audience. There is a fine line between presenting your information with confidence and finesse, and totally missing an opportunity to *"wow"* your audience. Prior to closing your presentation, allow a few minutes to take questions. And, if asked a question that you cannot answer, *don't fake it*. Respond appropriately, indicating that you will find out and get back with them as soon as possible. Most important, end with a memorable closing, usually a great supporting quote from a renowned leader helps round off your presentation.

- **Walk the room**. When presenting to small groups, using the opportunity to walk around the room is extremely effective. Periodically gaze across the entire room, using positive eye contact and smiling, as often as possible to convey a sense of confidence. Of course, walking the ballroom is not effective if you are presenting to a large group in the 100's because then everyone cannot see you. In these instances, stay on the stage or at the front of the room, periodically pacing from one side to the other to keep everyone's attention. When presenting to large groups, I prefer and always request a wireless microphone for this very reason.

- **Be mindful of the time.** If there is a clock in the room, glance at it from time to time to ensure you stay within the time allotted to you. I have been in meetings where the speaker went over their allocated time and participants started leaving. My suggestion, *respect people's time.* That's why handouts are so helpful. If you are running out of time, you can always advise participants to review the handouts later for more details.

#3 FEEDBACK FOR REFINEMENT *(After the Meeting)*
- **Solicit audience feedback.** The manner in which you solicit feedback depends on the audience you are presenting to. When I facilitate a training workshop, I always pass out participant feedback forms. When presenting to small groups, I speak with the meeting planner afterwards to get their feedback on the effectiveness of the presentation and suggestions for improvement.

- **Use feedback to improve your skills.** It's tough accepting constructive criticism and feedback when you have worked so hard preparing for a presentation or to facilitate a training workshop. However, you must take it all in stride and use what you learn to improve your presentation style. If you continue to hear the same criticism over-and-over again *(you use your hands to much, you pace too much, you let the audience take control too much, you didn't use eye contact with the audience, etc.)* then it is a chronic blind-spot that you need to work to eliminate. It's normal to be sensitive, but use this form of feedback as an opportunity to learn and grow over time. When you begin to hear the same criticisms *less* over time, you'll know that you have mastered your presentation skills.

Bottom-line, my list of tips for a powerful presentation is not all inclusive. However, hopefully it has gotten your creative juices going and in the future you will consider some of these tips to improve your presentation skills. There are hundreds of other tips to help you improve. I give hundreds of presentations each year, yet I still review books and other self-help resources to refine my skills. Believe me, your first, second, or maybe even fiftieth presentation will not be perfect – but the more presentations you do over time the more confident and effective you will become.

SUMMARY QUESTIONS

- *How will this information help you improve your presentation skills?*

- *What will you immediately start doing differently to improve your presentation skills?*

- *What impact might these changes have on your ability to communicate with a higher level confidence and credibility?*

Chapter 15

The Power of Professional Presence – The 20 Basics

Professional presence and image are cornerstones to career advancement and financial success. Studies show that 55% of other people's perception of you is based on your visual appearance, 38% is based on your tone of voice, and 7% based on the words you use.

These statistics prove that while sounding intelligent contributes to presenting a powerful image, other factors like appearance, nonverbal communication, proper etiquette and social graces are also key contributing factors.

Experts believe that you only have thirty seconds to make an impact on others. Many claim that within the first 30 seconds of interaction, others assume your *trustworthiness, level of education, job competence, ethnicity, sense of humor, and personality* – largely based on what they see, and all before you open our mouth.

Whether you are an entry level employee who aspires to move up the corporate ladder, or a manager seeking information to enhance your team's grooming and appearance standards, consider these twenty basics.

1. **Always take pride and care in your personal appearance, dress, and grooming.** This is essential to presenting a professional image at all times, and a positive, lasting impression.

2. **If your job requires you to wear a uniform, it should be well-maintained, clean, and pressed every day.** If your uniform is ripped, torn, or damaged, notify the proper individuals right away to have it repaired or replaced.

3. **Shoes should always be polished and in good condition.** For jobs requiring specific footwear, make it your priority to be in compliance to ensure safety and uniformity.

4. **Good hygiene is paramount to presenting a professional image.** It goes without saying, bathe or shower, use deodorant, and brush your teeth daily. You never want to give off body odor or breath that is offensive to others.

5. **Hair should always be clean, neat, and in a professional style.** Ladies, if you have long hair it should be pulled back away from your face. Gentlemen, your hair should be neatly trimmed at or above the standard collar line, unless otherwise specified by your company.

6. **Gentlemen, facial hair should be well-groomed.** Mustaches, beards or goatees *(if allowed)* should be neatly trimmed.

7. **Ladies, make-up should be tastefully applied.** Not excessive, especially eye-shadow and lipstick. Stay away from stark, glittery colors that may be distracting to others.

8. **Keep your fingernails neatly trimmed, clean and moderate in length.** Extreme decorations and length of nails can be distracting; ladies should wear moderate shades of nail polish with little or no nail art or jewelry.

9. **Remember, your name tag is a major part of your uniform.** If required for your job, name tags should be worn at all times, on your left side, approximately 2-3 inches below your collarbone.

10. **When it comes to jewelry, minimal is best.** Depending on the work environment, anything more than one pair of earrings, one watch and/or bracelet, one necklace, and two rings may be considered excessive.

11. **Body piercings and tattoos should be concealed and not visible while at work,** unless otherwise specified based on your work environment.

12. **Colognes and perfume should be used in moderation.** Keep in mind

some people have allergies that could be easy aggravated by your cologne or perfume smell.

13. **Always be mindful of your undergarments.** They should never be visible, even through your uniform.

14. **Chewing gum at work is unprofessional.** Instead, carry mints to ensure your breath is never offensive to others.

15. **Smile when talking on the telephone.** Your voice will sound more pleasant, alert, and receptive to what the other person is saying.

16. **Be mindful of your body language.** Standing alert, a genuine smile, positive eye contact, and a firm handshake all contribute to presenting a welcoming and confident professional image.

17. **The use of profanity at work is never acceptable,** especially in the presence of customers, clients, and co-workers. Keep in mind, what you say and how you say it can immediately diminish your image and respect within the work place.

18. **Practice proper table manners,** especially when attending social events for work. Remember, all eyes are on you, and in many cases, people are *judging your professionalism*, even as you take a second to eat a bite of food or to sip a beverage.

19. **Use proper grammar and vocabulary when conversing with customers, clients, and co-workers.** Conservation is a great way to build positive, lasting business relationships. Never dominate a conversation, but be mindful to listen more to ensure you understand the other person's perspective and leave them with a feeling of being valued and heard.

20. **Be an ambassador of your company, inside and outside of the workplace.** Always speak positively. Avoid gossip and negativity by immediately addressing such issues and concerns with the appropriate person.

Bottom-line, your ability to be promoted and move up the corporate ladder is just as contingent on presenting a professional image, as it is on being technically astute in your the job. If image is an issue that may be holding you back, start working on it today!

SUMMARY QUESTIONS

- *Which grooming and appearance issues do you need to work on to enhance your professional presence?*

- *Which grooming and appearance issues do you find difficult to enforce with your team?*

- *How might focusing on grooming and appearance issues increase the professionalism, effectiveness, and credibility of your team?*

Chapter 16

Confronting Unacceptable Behavior – The 8 Essentials

In the workplace, there are many times when a supervisor or manager simply cannot accept poor employee job performance. When leaders choose to do so, not only do they compromise the core values of the organization *(like treating all individuals with the highest levels of dignity and respect)*, but their credibility and ability to hold staff accountable also comes into question.

The longer poor or disruptive employee behavior is allowed to continue in the workplace, the more difficult it is for supervisors and managers to maintain a productive, harmonious work environment. Therefore, in order to demonstrate your effectiveness as a leader, poor or disruptive behavior cannot be tolerated or allowed to persist.

No one gets enjoyment out of having to pull an employee to the side to discuss their behavior; whether it's because the employee treated a customer poorly; was disrespectful to a co-worker; or was insubordinate to you as their leader. *Why?* Because most people don't like conflict and would rather turn a blind eye to the situation than risk the chance of being insulted if they confront the employee head on. The problem is that the longer you let these type situations go unfettered, the more the employee will challenge you in the future with even worse behavior. So, you must come to the realization that there is no alternative but to directly confront the issue in a professional manner.

To build your confidence and courage, here are eight essential tips for effectively confronting poor behavior.

1. **Address the issue immediately.** If you cannot address the issue right away, make sure you do so before the end of their shift when it is still fresh in both of your minds. Waiting until the next day will only make the situation worse, and give the employee an opportunity to say they don't know what you are talking about.

2. **Discuss the matter in private.** Never correct or counsel an employee concerning their job performance or behavior in public, in front of customers, or in the presence of other employees. If you do this will increase the chances of the situation escalating into a loud shouting match that may embarrass the both of you and affect employee morale, and your credibility. Tap the employee on the shoulder, find a vacant office or conference room, ask them to sit down, then explain specifically what the problem or issue is that needs correcting.

3. **Be very polite.** There is no need to be aggressive or disrespectful about the situation; you should see this as an opportunity to coach and counsel the employee to ensure improved performance. As they raise their voice, you should maintain a professional tone and remain calm.

4. **Allow them to respond.** Listen carefully to the employee's side, letting them talk *(for at most 10 minutes)* without interrupting. If the employee's tone becomes rude or disrespectful, you should pause and allow the employee to respond to your statements. Do not talk over them, do not return with abusive language, but also do not back down on your position.

5. **Don't take it personally.** There could be other reasons for the employee's aggression -- like personal issues outside of work, disregard of authority, or just plain jealousy. It's not your job to theorize why they are being aggressive; it is your responsibility to stick to the issue at hand. If the employee continues to be argumentative and disrespectful, bring the

conversation back to its original purpose and ask another manager to sit in on the remainder of the meeting.

6. **Explore solutions together.** Involve the employee in deciding what is needed to resolve the issue; this makes them just as accountable as you are for improved performance. If the poor or disrespectful behavior was a result of something that occurred in the workplace, suggest that in the future they come to you instead of taking it out on others. Show them that you care and that you are committed to their success, but that you cannot tolerate continued unacceptable behavior.

7. **Reinforce the behavior you want corrected.** Firmly, but politely reiterate *what the employee did wrong, why you are addressing it,* and *what are the consequences if it happens again.* Do not allow the employee to intimidate you. If this is the first time you have brought this to their attention the situation may warrant a verbal warning. However, if this issue has been addressed in the past with little or no improvement in their behavior – then it's time for a written warning that will go in their file.

8. **Notify senior leadership.** Make sure your Manager, Senior Leader, or Human Resource representative is aware of the incident so they are prepared if it escalates. This is why documenting the incident *(whether it's a verbal or written warning)* is the best policy. Long-term employees have a tendency to go above your head and complain about the counseling session, but if you follow proper protocol and handle the situation with a high level of professionalism you should have little to be concerned about.

Honestly, confronting unacceptable employee behavior in the workplace is not easy the *first, second,* or *third* time you have to do it. However, with time and experience your confidence and comfort level will certainly increase.

If employees believe that you will not hold them accountable for poor performance, they will not take you seriously as a leader.

In the final analysis, not confronting the issue with a sense of urgency not only hurts the employee's chances for growth and career advancement, but also damages your reputation within the organization. Following these tips for effectively confronting unacceptable behavior are not only guaranteed to help you help and your team grow and flourish, but also ensure that you create and sustain a productive, harmonious work environment.

SUMMARY QUESTIONS

- *When it comes to confronting unacceptable behavior in the workplace what are your weak points?*

- *How will strengthening these weak points improve your work environment?*

- *What impact will your ability to effectively confront poor behavior have on your overall effectiveness as a leader?*

Chapter 17

Delegation, Empowerment, and Time Management – The 5 Essentials

Few professionals feel that they typically have adequate time to get all of their routine tasks and priorities accomplished in a timely manner. As we all say, *"Time is not on my side."*

When you consider the concept of time management, there are many facets to effectively achieving it -- like work structure and organization; pacing yourself; listing your key priorities and using it as a guide; appropriate scheduling of your time, which is calendar management; and of course, knowing when and how to say *"no"* to additional, non-value adding tasks and projects.

However, the biggest key contributor to effective time management is delegation and employee empowerment. So, for the purposes of alignment and clarity, let us define both.

- **Delegation** is the assignment of authority and responsibility to another person *(normally from a manager to a subordinate)* to carry out specific job duties or tasks. However, the person who delegated the work remains accountable for the outcome of the delegated work.

- Delegation **empowers** a subordinate to make decisions, *i.e. it is a shift of decision-making authority from one organizational level to a lower one.* Delegation, if properly done, is not abdication. The opposite of effective delegation is micromanagement, where a manager provides too much input, direction, and review of delegated work.

- **Empowerment** is giving employees the freedom to make decisions without the authority of a manager or supervisor, after they have been properly trained.

When working with leaders to increase job performance, effectiveness, and business acumen, I often hear that they don't have time to delegate – simply because there is too much to be done and not enough time. This frequent excuse leads to a vicious circle that never ends unless the leader is willing to stop, re-evaluate their role and effectiveness, and make incremental changes in the way work gets done to improve the situation.

My five basics for effective time management are simple and outlined below. Before you consider a more sophisticated approach to managing your time I recommend you master these basics, because if you are not committed to these fundamental steps no new technology, computer software, or other calendar management tool or technique will work for you.

1. **Write everything down.** With so much you are accountable for accomplishing, why frustrate yourself? Less than 5% of the leadership population has a photographic memory. If you are not in that talented minority -- keep a notepad with you at all times to jot down specific requests and reminders. Not only does writing things down help you maintain self-accountability, integrity, and credibility -- it also helps

you effectively hold others accountable for tasks you have asked them to accomplish.

2. **Keep one calendar.** Too many leaders keep separate professional and personal/social calendars. *Talk about a time waster!* Keeping up with more than one calendar leads to double-bookings, as well as missed meetings, appointments, and commitments.

3. **Set monthly and weekly priorities.** Dedicate the last week of every month to proactively planning for the next month. Sunday afternoons are typically best for planning because you tend to be more relaxed and have a clear head. Monthly planning is the key to keeping perspective of the *"big picture"* and key initiatives that need to be accomplished by specific timelines. Monthly planning helps relieve the stress of having so much to do and so little time. Weekly planning helps you adjust and prioritize your schedule based on other competing or urgent priorities that may land on your desk during the month.

4. **Know when to say NO.** When you say *"yes"* to every single request, you disappoint almost everyone. Keep track of your commitments, and when you truly cannot accept another commitment or request, graciously apologize and explain why.

5. **Train and Delegate.** Take stock of all the tasks you typically have to accomplish within a given day or week, then determine which tasks can be delegated to other team members with proper training. Our studies show that managers often spend a good majority of their time doing tasks that their team could handle with just a little training and development.

Again, once you have mastered these five simple steps there are a myriad of time management tools and resources at your disposal.

Not properly managing your time leads to *multiple mistakes, inefficiencies* and *rework* that not only impacts your department, but sometimes the entire organization. It also leads to burn-out, a sense of being overwhelmed, and a lack of focus on those key issues that are important in steering the organization forward.

On the other hand, effective time management creates a sense of accomplishment, pride and joy in your work, and the development of your team. It means you can take time-off from work for personal renewal, and not have to worry if the office will go up in flames in your absence. Effective time management leads to proper delegation and the empowerment of your team, which demonstrates that you trust their judgments and have faith in their ability to properly perform their jobs.

The Flight of the Buffalo is an excellent leadership book and national bestseller that was written in 1993 by James Belasco and Ralph Stayer. In reading it, I gained insights on how to develop, empower and effectively delegate -- leading me to achieve greater goals. This book forces you to consider whether you run your team like a *"herd of buffalo"* or a *"flock of geese."* If you haven't read it and struggle with time management, as well as delegation and empowerment within your team, I urge you find the book and read it.

Summary Questions

- Which of the five basics of time management do you need to place the most emphasis on in improving your effectiveness as a leader?

- What tasks are you currently involved in that (with a little training and coaching) could be delegated to another employee on your team?

- How might proper delegation and employee empowerment impact employee engagement and customer loyalty within your organization?

Chapter 18

Interviewing with Excellence – The 10 Essentials

One of the keys to creating and sustaining a culture of service, performance, and operational excellence is selecting the right team that will enable you to raise the bar.

Too many leaders are not skilled in proper recruitment, interview, and selection techniques; therefore, they continuously make the same hiring mistakes over and over again. In the end not only does the organization suffer, but so does the customer to whom we are providing our products or services.

As a recruitment specialist for a world-renowned luxury hotel company for a number of years, I was able to experience first-hand how making the right choices in selecting top talent drove the organization from 60% labor turnover and moderate customer satisfaction, to single digit labor turnover and high customer loyalty. During that time I followed ten essentials that lead to international acclaim as an organization of excellence, national quality awards, as well as service and profit dominance in our industry.

1. **Create Alignment** – All leaders, supervisors, and other recruitment professionals within the organization must be aligned with the *key talents* and *characteristics* that are needed to drive and sustain organizational excellence. This ensures that everyone is consistently looking for the same employee profile and level of talent in filling their job openings. It also eliminates wasted time in the interview process with applicants who will not be a good *"fit"* for the organization. Beyond technical skills,

look for candidates who demonstrate a *sense of urgency;* have a *positive attitude;* are *natural smilers;* show up for the interview *well-groomed* and *appropriately attired;* and exhibit *attention to detail* in how their resume and application for employment is prepared.

2. **Use Structured Interview Questions** – Every aspect of the interview process should be carefully planned, starting with the preliminary screening, whether the interview is over the telephone or in-person. When an organization doesn't have structured interview questions that are consistently used by all hiring managers, it can lead to them asking questions which may be perceived as discriminatory or illegal in accordance with the EEOC. *If your organization doesn't have structured interview questions, there is a wealth of reliable information accessible via the internet to help you formulate well structured, legally sound interview questions.*

3. **Don't Rely Solely on Technology** – There's a lot of software, electronic resources and tools in the marketplace to make the selection of new employees more efficient. However, sometimes efficiency can be at the cost of losing great candidates who for one reason or another may have been weeded out by or because of technology. Definitely use technology as a resource, but integrate face-to-face interaction by scheduling open-application days, and participation in community job fairs to ensure you don't miss out on good talent that may not be technology savvy.

4. **Select for Skill AND Talent** – During the interview process, don't get too caught up in the candidate's impressive education, qualifications, and background without also assessing whether they have natural talents *(like positivity, caring, attention to detail, team player, empathy, sense of urgency, organization skills, high work ethic, etc.)*, as these may also be qualities that are needed to ensure organizational success.

5. **Hold Out for the BEST** – Don't compromise the established hiring standards of your organization or team because you are short-staffed. Holding out for the best demonstrates a higher level of loyalty to your team and the organization. Hiring warm bodies *(reactionary hiring vs. proactive hiring)* will only contribute to increased problems in the work environment down the road.

6. **Integrate Team Interviews** – Getting a second opinion is a great way to ensure you are making the right hiring decision. Whenever possible, select 1-2 exemplary individuals from your team to meet with the job candidate; have prepared questions for them to ask; and confer after the interview to get a good read on the candidate. The team may see qualities *(good or bad)* that somehow you overlooked. Team involvement increases accountability and commitment to ensuring the success of the new employee.

7. **Select an Interview Tool that Works for Your Organization** – Structured questions that have been created by an HR professional within your organization are a great start, because it's far better than just asking an applicant questions off-the-cuff. However, highly effective organizations select a behavioral interview tool that is carefully researched, legally validated, and will ensure they select only the best and brightest talent. In the past I used Talent+ with great success, and highly recommend you Google them. However, there are a number of organizations that specialize in this area that might be equally effective for your organization.

8. **Be Accountable** – Hold yourself and others involved in the selection process accountable for good hires. No leader should be allowed to hire any employee that they would not stand 100% behind. Being accountable in this capacity goes hand-in-hand with *Essential #5* – Holding out for the best talent.

9. **Be Prepared** – Always be ready going into an interview. You will most likely represent the first impression of your organization, and if it is an impression of disorganization and chaos the candidate will make that assumption of the entire organization. Being prepared means that: you have familiarized yourself with the candidate's resume and application; you have reviewed your list of interview questions to ask; you have reserved a quiet, neat and organized location to meet with them; you have scheduled an appropriate amount of uninterrupted time so the interview doesn't seemed rushed; you are prepared to give them a thorough explanation of the job they are applying for and what to expect; and you can intelligently explain the next steps in the selection process for them.

10. **Ensure Timely Follow-Up** – Set and communicate a realistic timeline for follow-up with applicants to eliminate continuous telephone calls and email inquiries from them concerning the job and interview. For non-skilled job openings, applicants should be advised of the status of their application within 7-10 working days. For job openings that required a higher level of technical skill, education, and leadership experience, 30 days is appropriate. If you need more time to make a hiring decision, out of courtesy, make contact with the applicant to advise them.

Bottom-line, just as job candidates are aware that they need to make a lasting first impression during their interview, the same goes for the interviewer. The preparation invested *before, during,* and *after* the interview speaks volumes about an organization.

SUMMARY QUESTIONS

- *Does your current interview and selection process set you up for success?*

- *If no, what are some things that you are committed to changing to ensure you select and retain top talent within your team?*

- *How might improving your interview skills impact service, performance, and operational excellence for the organization as a whole?*

Chapter 19

Driving Results with a Lean Staff – The 15 Essentials

Working with a reduced number of staff during lean financial times can be either a blessing in disguise or a curse, depending on your outlook. For those of you who are working with limited staff due to budget cuts, reductions in force, or lean quality initiatives – here are 15 simple tips to help you achieve optimum results.

1. **Keep the flow of communication open.** With limited staff and resources, effective listening and communication is vital to success. If you don't keep your team regularly updated, you leave the work environment open to negative gossip, rumors, and speculation that may be far from the truth.

2. **Create a high sense of trust.** The quickest way to build trust is to demonstrate your loyalty to your team. When employees feel that you trust them and their judgment, they are more apt to go above and beyond to ensure the team's success.

3. **Solicit good ideas.** Don't operate in a vacuum; solicit good ideas from staff members on how to improve efficiencies within the department. Then involve them in determining which ideas get implemented, tracked and measured for success. When you sincerely ask, with the intent of using their input to improve the work environment, it is amazing the positive feedback you will receive from staff.

4. **Reward and recognize.** Even the smallest victories should be acknowledged, showing your appreciation for a job well done. When you are working with a lean staff, be sure to give them as much credit publicly as possible for system improvements. And don't forget, a sincere *"thank you"* at the end of the day will go miles in fostering employee engagement, trust and loyalty.

5. **Create a culture of teamwork.** Create a *"we"* mentality through teamwork and self-accountability. When working with a lean staff, employees who don't feel they are part of a team can quickly erode workplace morale and job satisfaction. Reward and recognize *team achievements* as much as possible to reinforce the need for everyone to be a valued contributor to team success.

6. **Create a culture of empowerment.** Empowerment is giving employees the freedom and authority to make workplace decisions, after they have been properly trained. Trust is a by-product of employee empowerment. So make time to ensure the staff is properly cross-trained, and equipped with the skill and knowledge to make sound decisions on your behalf.

7. **Focus on process improvement.** Identify ways to streamline work processes, so they are more efficient, save time, and enhance the product or service you provide. When working with a lean staff, it's critical that systems and processes are refined to eliminate mistakes, rework, breakdowns, inefficiencies, and variations that create frustration and negativity in the workplace.

8. **Accelerate change.** This is not the time to be slothful. Change must happen *effectively, quickly,* and *with a high level of intensity*. The longer you wait to implement changes in the way work gets done, the more time you will allow for negativity to contaminate the work environment.

9. **Informally measure satisfaction.** Find cost-effective, low tech ways to assess the satisfaction of your internal and external customers.

Comment cards can be used for customers, and possibly some form of anonymous feedback like suggestion boxes for employees. Whatever process you use to get the information, be certain to *do something with it* – don't just gather the information for the sake of gathering it.

10. **Face the facts.** Honestly, change and innovation are the only way your organization or team will survive in lean times. Help your team realistically and positively face the fact that change is both inevitable and good.

11. **Encourage cross-training.** In lean times, it is vital that team members are capable of multi-tasking in a variety of roles. With accelerated change, comes the opportunity to learn new skills that may later lead to new and exciting career advancement opportunities. The more equipped your team is during lean times, the more they will be perceived as valued contributors within the organization.

12. **Encourage balance.** During lean times, staff members sometimes push themselves into a frenzy to get things done. This can lead to burn-out, low productivity, attendance issues, and low worker morale. So, be concerned and cautious of too much overtime, making sure staff members take their allotted lunch and breaks to ensure work-life balance.

13. **Respect the company.** Don't encourage or allow negativity to fester within the team. In the beginning most employees are negative about working with a lean staff. However, over time as work systems and processes become more efficient they will no longer miss the additional bodies that staffed the department. Be the role model by supporting the company's decision to operate with a lean team. If you cannot support and respect the company's decision, consider seeking other employment.

14. **Handle workplace conflict right away.** With the same level of intensity that you use in driving change during lean circumstances, you must also

quickly move to resolve internal conflict. In the beginning tensions may be high, but that is no reason to allow conflict to fester and eventually become uncontrollable. So don't avoid any inkling of conflict, confront and resolve it right away.

15. **View lean as permanent.** Don't consider having a lean staff as a temporary fix until the company's financial or strategic picture changes, otherwise the team will eventually revert back to their old, inefficient way of doing things. View lean as the *new way that work gets done*, encouraging the team to foster a work environment of continuous improvement.

Bottom-line, leaders are expected to drive results even in times when they are working with a lean staff. Certainly, teams who are able to create and sustain a culture of service, performance, and operational excellence under such circumstances will achieve success over the long-term.

SUMMARY QUESTIONS

- *Which of the fifteen essentials for driving results apply to your work environment?*

- *How might you use this information to improve team accountability, productivity and performance?*

- *How might applying these fifteen essentials impact organizational success?*

Chapter 20

Overcoming Tough Economic Times – The Ten Imperatives

At some point in time, most leaders will face either an economic downturn in their industry or a global recession. While only a select few can 100% protect their businesses from an impending economic decline, there are some things we can do to proactively position our organization favorably.

If faced with an economic slowdown, before you start eliminating customer amenities that make your product or service distinct and competitive in the market, before increasing your prices or mass layoffs, take into account the following strategic imperatives to recession-proofing your business.

1. **Streamline and refine work processes** – By applying quality improvement methods, have every department or business unit identify ways to get work done better, faster, and more cost-efficient. Getting employees involved in the process will help you more effectively and expediently identify breakdowns, rework, mistakes, inefficiencies, and variations in the workplace. These are the issues that may be contributing to wasted time and money, lost productivity, and potential employee and customer dissatisfaction.

2. **Set realistic business objectives** – Review current productivity, revenue and sales data, and then solicit each department or business unit to develop a simple strategy to reduce their expenses by 10%-15%.

Before the department looks at cutting staffing levels, they should identify other budgetary line items like labor overtime, office supplies, equipment upgrades *(that could be delayed)*, energy consumption, and business travel. These are just a few examples, have every manager review their budget and the monthly P&L for specifics that are applicable to your line of business.

3. **Identify and cut low performers** - If ever, this is not a good time to hold on to low to poor performers. If employee performance reviews have *not* been done in a consistent and fair manner over the past 2-3 years, doing so without potential legal retribution will be difficult. On the other hand, if your organization has employed a comprehensive, consistent, and fair performance review process that every leader is held to the highest accountability level for conducting, this will be no problem. In tough economic times, it costs your company vital time and money to retain the bottom 10% *(low performers)*.

4. **Increase customer service** – This is not the time to allow customer service to lag behind, be conscientious of it every day. During slow economic times, customers are more discerning about how they spend their money; and while they will be looking for discount deals, the level of service is still equally important in maintaining their loyalty. The little things like consistently using the customer's name, saying *"thank you"* and *"please"*, serving customers with a sense of urgency, anticipating customer needs before they have to ask, all contribute to making the customer feel valued. In the final analysis, when customers feel valued, they are more likely to become loyal to your product or service.

5. **Innovate** – This is a great time to reconsider new markets and new customers that you hadn't thought of before. Form a small team of exemplary employees from sales, operations, administration, etc. Include senior leaders, mid-managers, and line level staff members. Ask them to brainstorm on innovative, out-of-the-box, cost-efficient ways

to attract new customers and increase the current customer-base. Not all of the ideas will be realistic or implementable; however, it only takes one or two new ideas to significantly jump start business, revenue, and ultimately, profitability.

6. **Create a "Game Plan"** – Having a sound strategy in place demonstrates that your organization is serious about improving efficiencies to achieve cost-savings, while ensuring you stay the course and maintain a competitive advantage. Keep it simple. Don't create a game plan that is exhaustive and causes so much extra work that staff members become negative about it. Your game plan should be realistic, measurable, and communicate timelines by which key benchmarks must be attained.

7. **Step up Employee Communication** – One of the most fatal mistakes leaders make during tough economic times is not keeping employees updated. Frequent communication in the form of blogs, morning briefings, newsletters... are a great opportunity to align staff with the current economic conditions, what the organization is doing to overcome it, and to rally employee support and active participation in a winning game plan.

8. **Retool employees** – The way that work gets done in tough economic times is different from when we are experiencing a robust economy. Make sure employees are equipped with the motivation, skill, and knowledge to properly resolve customer problems, to effectively accomplish more with less people, and to identify and implement effective ways to ensure cost-savings. This is not a time to cut employee learning and development out altogether, but it is a prime opportunity to re-evaluate how learning occurs, and to determine if it is focused on equipping employees to meet and achieve business demands. While we recommend reducing the amount of classroom training that occurs during tough economic times, we strongly encourage stepping up the use of departmental meetings,

web-based training, and other internal resources as an opportunity to enhance learning and development.

9. **Increase leadership accountability** – This reinforces the significance of the matter. If employees and managers see this initiative as one that will fade off of the radar screen within a matter of weeks, they won't take it seriously. The best way to ensure sustainability are through routine checks to follow-up and make sure all departments or business units are adhering to the established game plan, that they are tracking successes and failures, reacting and improving as needed.

10. **Celebrate Small Victories** - Just because the organization is in cost containment mode does not mean we should neglect recognizing exemplary behavior and the extraordinary support of employees, through some form of reward. Even when small victories or key goals are achieved, either by an individual contributor or a team, there is room for celebration. In essence, when staff members have sacrificed the conveniences of additional team members, maybe even fewer supplies and other resources to ensure the organization can financially weather the storm, it is a leadership obligation to show appreciation in some manner. Even non-monetary recognition like a brief, handwritten *"thank you"* note or letter from leadership will go a long way.

To make it through tough economic times with few scratches and bruises, your organization must have a sound strategy. It does not happen by chance. While these ten strategic imperatives may not alleviate our company all together from the economic crunch, it will display that leadership is doing everything possible to maintain the integrity of the business, retain valuable employees and customers, and sustain a culture of service, performance, and operational excellence.

Most of all, while this list of ten strategic imperatives is not all inclusive, our hope is that it starts you on the track of creatively looking at ways to weather the economic storm, and bring your team through it with a high level of support and anticipation that there will be a light at the end of the tunnel.

Bottom-line, I am not giving you suggestions that have not been tested. Years ago I worked for an organization that was on the brink of financial ruin due largely to the impact of the 9/11 terrorist attacks. We employed all of these practices, and many others. While hard decisions had to be made that impacted the lives of many leaders and employees alike, the morale that we came out of the circumstances with where exceptionally higher than that of our competitors.

SUMMARY QUESTIONS

- *Which of the ten imperatives for overcoming tough economic times have you applied in the past?*

- *What worked /didn't work?*

- *What would you do differently, if placed in this situation again?*

Chapter 21

Top 5 Mistakes Managers Make in Recessionary Times

During difficult economic times, keeping the team aligned, positive, and focused on creating excellence can be quite challenging. Managers with a short-term mentality tend to have more difficulty because they focus solely on the current state of things. In contrast, highly effective leaders have more of a long-term outlook and subsequently are more capable of helping their team weather the storm.

To prevent you from getting short-sighted, here are my top five mistakes to avoid or stop doing in recessionary times:

1. **Not focusing on inefficiencies in the workplace** - The first red flag that should arise during tough economic times are inefficiencies within the workplace that not only waste valuable time, resources, and money – but also create a high level of employee frustration due to mistakes and rework. Before you start cutting people, services, equipment or other resources, you should quickly surface and improve systems and processes that create inefficiencies. Surprisingly, you may find that additional staff has been hired *(year-after-year)* to work around the inefficiencies, instead of just resolving and eliminating them forever.

2. **Cutting services without proper rationale** - When it comes to cost cutting measures, short-term minded managers are quick to cut services and amenities that the customer has become accustomed to, often without doing any preliminary fact checking. This is not to say that if a

complimentary service or amenity is a *"nice to have,"* but creates no value in the way of customer loyalty that we should keep it. We are only saying, do your research before such cuts are implemented to ensure they don't create a backlash of customer dissatisfaction.

3. **Reducing internal communication** - During tough economic times, employee communication should be accelerated, not brought to a screeching halt or worst, eliminated. However, for no apparent reason managers tend to communicate less with their team during tough economic times – rarely updating them on the financial state of affairs within the organization. Managers view this as *"no news is good news,"* while employees view it as the exact opposite, *"no news is bad news."*

4. **Eliminating employee training** – Certainly a recession is no time to ramp up spending on unnecessary training programs that are non-value adding to the organization. However, it is also not the right environment for cutting employee learning and development altogether. Without proper communication and training, employee focus quickly shifts to negativity. Value-added training that reinforces *customer service, service recovery, departmental cross-training,* and *workplace safety* will equip your team with the skills and knowledge to continue creating a memorable experience for every customer – whether they call into your office, enter your doors, or visit your website.

5. **Drastically slashing prices** - Even with good service, some companies may still need to re-evaluate their pricing strategy to maintain competitiveness. However, before doing so here are a few questions to ponder. *Realistically, in a sluggish economy does it make sense for customers to use us instead of a competitor who charges less? Does our product or service live up to its promise enough to hold tight on our pricing? Instead of cutting our pricing or fees, can we offer additional amenities or services that are perceived as a high-value to the customer, yet low-cost (if any cost at all) to*

us? Just do your research before you start slashing prices, because it may not be so easy increasing your prices when the recession ends.

Bottom-line, a sound action plan forces you to make the right decisions before cutting products and services. It forces you to restructure your pricing strategy to maximize results. It enables you to identify and eliminate inefficiencies in the workplace that are creating waste. And most of all, integrates effective employee communication and cross-training in the midst of lean staffing to ensure financial viability. So, assuming you have a plan in place – use it!

SUMMARY QUESTIONS

- *Which of the top five mistakes have you made in the past?*

- *How did that decision impact your organization or team?*

- *Based on what we have covered, what would you do differently the next time around?*

Part 3
Human Resource, Employee Learning & Development

Chapter 22

Fifteen Standards Every HR Department Should Live By

As a Performance Consultant, I spend a good amount of time with Human Resource and Learning & Development professionals. As a matter of fact, prior to starting my consulting firm I was an executive with The Ritz-Carlton Hotel Company, in both disciplines. With close to twenty years of service with The Ritz-Carlton organization, I feel very qualified to share a few simple standards of excellence that every Human Resource team should exemplify.

Whether you are a one-person HR operation, or have a squadron of HR professionals working for you, what is most essential is the manner in which your customers *(the employees)* are treated.

A highly effective, productive HR operation creates a work environment that is employee-centered. Not one where employees are perceived as an *interruption* to getting paperwork and rudimentary task accomplished. Great HR professionals focus on fostering a work environment that makes the organization a great place to work.

To ensure you stay focused on the customer *(your employees)*, never assume that your HR team knows what is necessary to drive excellence without first clarifying it. Again, whether you are a one-person operation or have a team of HR professionals, listed below are the primary standards of performance, excellence and professionalism that should set the tone for every HR team.

1. Keep the company philosophy alive! Assist all employees through open communication, training and role modeling to ensure they understand how to *exemplify* service excellence every day.

2. Extend genuine care by being *warm, personable, sincere, compassionate,* and *approachable* in your interactions with staff; instilling a sense of value and well-being in each employee.

3. Greet employees and job applicants with a *warm welcome*. Set the example with smiles and positive eye contact, using names when possible, and always use proper telephone etiquette.

4. Promote an Open Door Policy with all employees whenever possible.

5. Create an atmosphere of teamwork and positivity in the department, and throughout the Company.

6. Any Human Resource representative who receives a question, inquiry or complaint *owns it* and will follow through to completion. Always demonstrate a sense of urgency when addressing employee issues, and in following through on their ideas, suggestions, and concerns.

7. Treat all employee records and incidents with a high degree of respect, professionalism and confidentiality.

8. Create awareness of safety in the workplace; assist in the training of all employees with regard to safety and emergency procedures. Job safety and security will be constantly emphasized to make our work environments safe for our customers to visit and for our employees to work in.

9. All applicants will be properly recruited and hired through a structured hiring and selection process.

10. All new employees will receive an in-depth orientation BEFORE starting work, with a follow-up session after 30-days of employment.

11. When possible, open positions will be first offered to current staff members to maximize internal succession planning, career growth, and employee development.

12. All managers will participate in at least two leadership learning and development activities per year. New employees will have a structured training schedule in each department.

13. Our Company will be recognized as the best to work for and where work is exciting! Employee reward and recognition programs will be designed to foster high morale and positive attitude.

14. Our compensation and benefits package will be comparable to competitors within the area.

15. All employees will be certified annually through job specific training, insisting on 100% compliance.

Bottom-line, HR plays a significant role in impacting employee engagement, satisfaction, and retention. If practiced with a high level of commitment and consistency, the standards outlined above will set your HR operation on the road to being a valued contributor to the success of the organization. Good luck!

SUMMARY QUESTIONS

- *What are some of the standards of excellence that your HR Team is currently responsible for demonstrating?*

- *Based on what we have shared, what would you add?*

- *If your HR Team exemplified this type behavior every day, how would it impact employee engagement, the work environment, and the success of your organization?*

Chapter 23

Gaining the Support of Your C-Level – The 5 Essentials

How can learning and development professionals best align their work with the needs of their C-Level Executives or the Board? Well, I have been doing this for many years; first as Human Resource and Training professional with The Ritz-Carlton Hotel Company, then as a Performance Consultant with my own firm.

The Five Essentials

1. **Organizational Priorities** - understand their business goals and objectives. Learn what's keeping them up at night; what are their key priorities *(organizational growth, improved profits, customer loyalty, or improved efficiencies).*

2. **Strategize** – create a talent development strategy that is linked to the achievement of the organizational priorities and to their goals. This will build your credibility among C-Level executives and demonstrate your interest in partnering with them to close organizational gaps that are limiting the achievement of key goals. Your strategy should include *what* you plan to do, *who* will be involved, *when* it will be accomplished, and *which* key priorities it will impact.

3. **Communication & Involvement** – share your strategy and solicit their feedback and input. Be careful not to go into unnecessary specifics concerning the plan, but do have details accessible in case you are

asked to expound further. Most C-Level executives are not particularly interested in *how* you will execute the plan, but *what it will improve and when*. This is also an excellent time to solicit their help as a champion, advocate, or active participant.

4. **PILOT & REFINE** – pilot the program *(incorporating the involvement of your C-Level champions)* before implementing it system-wide. Then share key findings from the pilot program, tweaking it as needed based on comments from participating C-Level executives.

5. **MEASURE AND QUANTIFY** – consider how you will quantify the ROI *(return on investment)* of your talent development strategy and programs, and what you will measure to determine success. With the launch of your strategy, will the organization experience *increased efficiencies, customer loyalty, cost-savings,* or *employee retention*? When you can quantify success and back it up with a realistic plan of action, you will easily gain their ear and support.

Bottom-line, in order to align your work with the needs of C-Level executives or Board Members, you must think like them by focusing on a strategy that will help eliminate pressing business issues that may be keeping them up at night. In the final analysis, not only will you be perceived as a valued contributor to the organization, but if your learning and development or talent management endeavors are successful, the likelihood of career advancement may be eminent.

SUMMARY QUESTIONS

- *How supportive are senior executives and/or Board Members of your HR and Training initiatives?*

- *Based on what we have shared, which of the five essentials might be beneficial in helping you get HR and Training initiatives endorsed by senior leadership?*

- *How might applying these five essentials impact your effectiveness and credibility as an HR or Training Professional?*

Chapter 24

The Top Ten Ways to Recruit and Retain Highly Talented Employees

Few leaders can create and sustain a culture of *service, performance,* and *operational excellence* without a highly skilled and talented workforce rallying behind them. If you find yourself in a situation where you need to rebuild your team, or strengthen their performance capability to meet business demands, then consider these top ten tips for recruiting and retaining top talent.

1. **Always be on the lookout for good talent.** The mistake too many managers and human resource professionals make is that they don't proactively search for new talent. This means keeping an eye out for good talent, even when there are no open positions. By doing so, you can create a *"talent bank"* of highly skilled people whom you can call on for interviewing when there is a need. If you only interview when there is a need within the company, your recruitment practices are reactive, ineffective, and may result in you continually spinning your wheels to find the right people. This is what often causes leaders to compromise in talent selection due to the urgency to fill an opening.

2. **Create a work environment that attracts highly skilled and talented people.** Just as *"word of mouth"* is the best advertisement any company can receive, the same adage holds true when recruiting good people. Employees love to brag about their jobs to others, and when they feel that they have an exceptional work environment they become your greatest

allies in the war on recruitment. Why do you think so many companies aspire to be part of the *"Great Place to Work"* list each year? Many will move heaven and earth to get on the list because the PR and notoriety it brings to the organization is invaluable when it comes to attracting the best and brightest candidates in the market. Your Employee Satisfaction Survey results are also a great indicator of whether your organization is a great place to work, and if the data suggests it I highly recommend you use this to your advantage.

3. **Create a work environment that also retains good talent.** I know of quite a few organizations that do an exceptional job of getting great talent in the door, *only to see them leave before twelve months have expired.* The best and brightest are often looking for a challenge in their career. To retain them you must offer an exceptional learning and development experience that will provide them with the skill and knowledge to continually move up the professional ladder. No one wants to stay with an organization that is stagnant, with no compelling vision or mission, and no opportunity to grow. Even if your organization is small, if growth is on the horizon there is no reason not to have a MIT *(manager in training)* or an internship program that will set the stage for a fulfilling, long-term career within your organization.

4. **Implement a robust Employee Referral Incentive Program.** The best applicants are typically those who are referred by existing employees. Especially in a tight labor markets, this is a program you should already have in place. Employee Referral Programs are typically more effective than posting job ads on websites. Most organizations pay $500 to $1000 to employees who refer exceptional applicants who are hired; with some stipulations. The new hires must stay with the company for at least 6-12 months before the referring employee gets all of the money, which forces them to refer good people who will stay with the company for a while. Bottom line, many organizations have Employee Referral Programs,

but they are so poorly marketed and executed that the return is often lackluster.

5. **Build a strong network with local universities, community colleges, and outreach organizations.** Forming an alliance within your community could ensure that you have others watching for good talent for you. Years ago when I worked with The Ritz-Carlton, we'd do special things for our key recruitment contacts within the community to stay in touch with them and show our appreciation. Our pool of recruitment resources included several local vocational schools, universities and high schools with hospitality programs, and a variety of religious and social services organizations. We would either take our contacts out for lunch or arrange a nicely catered lunch at our Hotel for them so we could reconnect. Then upon receiving our weekly list of job openings, we were first and foremost in their minds. We also made sure those in our recruitment network were clear on the caliber of applicants we were looking for, so they usually sent us the cream of the crop. Regularly showing that we appreciated their assistance paid off big, as they provided us with a constant stream of eligible candidates and students seeking work.

6. **Market your company's career and training opportunities everywhere you can.** Does your website have a page that is dedicated to glorifying the benefits of working for your organization? Or is it just another lackluster webpage that only lists job openings? Are updated career opportunities posted companywide, in areas that are visible and accessible to all employees? Does your company newsletter and intranet recognize employees who do an exemplary job of referring highly-quality applicants? Are your Employee Handbook and other internal employee oriented materials used to promote your Employee Referral Program, as well as career and growth opportunities within the organization? If the answer is *no*, you are missing out on simple ways to spread the word.

7. **Design and implement a structured recruitment and selection process.** When there is no process or strategy, success is unlikely. All of the ideas I have shared so far make up a sound recruitment and selection strategy. Once you have developed the strategy, get all of your leaders onboard and hold them accountable by not allowing any compromise in the process. An organization that has its act together concerning recruitment and selection typically has a written SOP *(standard operating procedure)* that everyone follows to the letter. There is little room for deviation because the process has been tried, tested and refined to ensure success. Your strategy and SOP should clarify from start to finish what the recruitment and selection experience should consist of, including the interview questionnaire or tool everyone should be using, and other pertinent forms that should be uniform throughout the organization.

8. **Build your bench internally.** Too often exceptional talent within the organization is overlooked because there is no time to develop, coach, and mentor. I refer to this segment of the workforce as *"diamonds in the rough."* With the effort and time invested in looking outside of the organization for talent, you could also be dedicating time to strengthening the talent within. Are you using IDPs *(individual development plans)* to surface internal talent, find out what they aspire for their career, and to determine what is necessary to help them get there? I can recall early in my Hotel career being overlooked because the General Manager was more focused in bringing in talent from the European hotel schools. Nothing against this concept, I think it adds flair and diversity to the organization. But please don't forget about the regular employees who make things happen every day, who are already within your organization and yearning to be *recognized, mentored, developed* and *promoted*. I eventually rose to a Vice President in Human Resources because someone noticed my talent and commitment.

9. **Don't settle for the** *"warm body"* **syndrome.** It's easy for leaders to become disillusioned, and out of desperation compromise the level of talent the organization needs in order to succeed. Remember, the more mediocre employees you hire into the organization, the less likely exemplary talent will want to work for you. Smart, motivated employees like to work with people who are similar – not with slackers. Stay attuned to the quality of employees *(good or bad)* that your managers and supervisors are bringing into the organization.

10. **Provide competitive benefits and wages.** Competitive wages and benefits certainly contribute to getting highly quality candidates in the door; however it will not keep them if the work environment is lousy. The best and brightest candidates have a lot of choices, and if your organization stands any chance in the labor market you cannot sell them short compensation-wise. Stay attuned with what your competitors are doing, and then create a strategy to stay aligned with them and eventually exceed what they offer. In the long term, the return on the investment in having a highly competitive compensation and benefits package will be realized in greater employee productivity and retention.

Now that you've reviewed some of the simple things that highly effective organizations do to recruit and retain exceptional employees, take a moment to assess your organization. On a scale of 1-5, with 5 high, how would you rate your organization? Next, determine what your leadership team must START, STOP, and CONTINUE doing to take recruitment and selection to the next level. You see, it's not enough to simply know what is necessary to drive excellence within an organization; you must also implement the things necessary to bring it to fruition.

Bottom-line, you must recruit the right people and create the right work environment!

SUMMARY QUESTIONS

- *Do you feel you have the right team members onboard to drive excellence?*

- *As you bring new team members onboard, what have you learned that could help you attract and retain the best and brightest talent in the market?*

- *If you apply some of the best practices shared, how would it positively impact your organization?*

Chapter 25

Creating Training that Sticks – The Top 10 Tips

More than ever when approving funding for major employee learning and development initiatives, senior leaders are concerned as to whether or not it will stick. With many years of employee training and executive development experience under my belt, there are ten tips that I have used with great success to create training that is *effective, memorable,* and *sustainable.*

1. **Solicit Employee Input.** To ensure training sticks, start by obtaining preliminary employee feedback before the training begins. Ask what they know about the company; its potential gaps in achieving established goals and objectives. Never assume they know everything that you know. Find out from their perspective how learning and development could improve their work environment and productivity, what they would like to get out of the learning, and what will make learning more interesting for them. Then customize the training content to meet not only the needs of the organization, but also those of its participants.

2. **Integrate Icebreakers.** To get everyone's creative juices flowing and jumpstart participant engagement, start the training session with a brief icebreaker that is relevant to the content that will be covered. The resource book, GAMES TRAINERS PLAY, includes hundreds of icebreaker ideas to choose from.

3. **Incorporate Storytelling.** Use real life stories and common examples to make key points relevant. An example might be that if you are facilitating

a workshop on Problem Resolution and Empowerment, use personal stories that illustrate a time when you received poor customer service and how it was resolved. You could even share personal examples of situations when you either felt empowered or disempowered to resolve an issue, citing specifically *who, what, where, and how* you overcame the situation with professionalism and finesse.

4. **Encourage Participant Involvement.** Actively engage participants throughout the learning process with open-ended questions, allowing them sufficient time to respond. We all learn when everyone participates; and as a workshop facilitator it demonstrates that you are on top of your game, comfortable sharing the spotlight with workshop participants, and that everyone is accountable for making the learning *energizing, inspiring, informative, fun,* and *memorable.*

5. **Use Visual Aids.** When possible, incorporating videos or PowerPoint presentations with relevant graphics are great way to stimulate the learning process. Also, proper use of a flipchart to jot down participant responses to illustrate or make a point adds variety to the learning process.

6. **Use Humor.** Interjecting funny stories that relate to the points you are making during the training are a great way to keep participants engaged and help them retain critical tips on things you want them to do or not do. Just make sure to keep all humor professional and in good taste.

7. **Discuss Life Application.** End training sessions by having participants share how they will apply what they have learned. This will encourage *self-reflection, self-accountability,* and *self- motivation* to use the tools, skills, and knowledge gained.

8. **Give Away Prizes.** You would be surprised how effective inexpensive giveaways *(like candy bars, movie tickets, small toys and trinkets, or books)* are in engaging participants and stimulating enthusiasm in learning.

Experience shows that when participants are fully engaged, they retain and apply a great deal of what they have learned.

9. **Incorporate Testing.** Give a brief quiz at the end of the training session to ensure retention of vital information. When participants believe they will be tested on the information covered, they are more likely to retain and later utilize what they have learned.

10. **Follow-Up.** Inform participants that you will be following up on their progress, and then do so to heighten self-accountability. Learning and development professionals who routinely follow-up with their participants are more successful in creating an environment where employees feel compelled to implement what they have learned.

Bottom-line, the key to creating training that sticks is engaging the learner in the process from start to finish. It is up to the workshop facilitator to ensure the learning sticks; therefore, they should build sustainability mechanisms into the training content and session. If you are a senior leader, make it a priority to let your learning professionals know that you will be following-up and expecting them to create a learning environment that will create sustainable change. Anything less is unacceptable.

SUMMARY QUESTIONS

- *Which tips for creating training that sticks will you immediately begin to apply?*

- *What tips would you add to the list?*

- *If you are able to create a learning environment where the training sticks, how would it positively impact your organization?*

Chapter 26

Getting the Most Out of Web-based Training

Web-based training is an excellent way to reinforce and augment most aspects of employee learning and development; especially when budget limitations make it hard to offer traditional classroom training for employees on a regular basis.

For some organizations, web-based training is not effective, while for others it is thriving. To ensure you get the most out of any web-based training program you embark on, here are ten best practices.

1. **Limit online workshops to no more than 10-20 minutes in duration.** In today's frantic work environment, it is almost impossible to sit in front of a computer for more than 20 minutes without being pulled away by a telephone call, another employee or customer needing assistance, or an urgent request from a boss. So minimizing the time helps! I can't think of anyone who enjoys online classes that last 30 minutes or more. Secondly, the attention span as well as retention rate of online courses that are longer than 20 minutes is extremely low, especially when no specific rewards like certification or CEUs are linked to taking the class.

2. **Limit the number of online workshops that are rolled-out each month or quarter.** Typically, when a multitude of online workshops are available at one time, the level of participation and interest drops. Years ago, my previous employer rolled out a robust web-based leadership development program that offered over 500 workshops, which appeared

to be impressive. However, less than 10% of managers participated because the selection of topics was just too much. Organizations that attain a 100% ROI with web-based training strategically introduce 3-5 new workshops each quarter.

3. **Develop a marketing campaign to roll-out the program.** At least two months before the online training program is rolled out it should be promoted to communicate its purpose, gain buy-in, and support. The marketing campaign should outline how the program will enhance the effectiveness of each participant, as well as how it will impact organizational success. It should also outline the types of courses that will be available, when and how they will be accessible, and how leaders who excel in the program will be recognized.

4. **Reward and Recognize successful completion.** Publicly recognize participants with certificates of completion, photos in the company newsletter or on your *wall of fame*, in leadership meetings, or with handwritten congratulatory notes from your CEO, HR Director or CLO *(chief learning officer)*. Organizations that achieve a significant ROI don't perceive this responsibility as a waste of time, but an opportunity to recognize employees who take self-accountability for enhancing their professional development.

5. **Outsource the content development.** Creating an engaging, value-adding, web-based training curriculum involves the expertise of many people *(a project manager, several subject matter experts, an instructional designer, IT specialist, etc.)*. Outsourcing content development responsibility frees you up to run your business with little obstruction of time. Be careful to select a vendor or supplier who can customize the program to meet your unique business needs, not just sell you off-the-shelf content. Not all online courses require customization; however, if that's your preference it should be an option that does not cost a tremendous amount of money.

6. **Allow participants downtime at work to complete online classes.** Research shows that in organizations who achieve a significant ROI with web-based training, 61% of participants are allowed downtime to take the courses while at work. Even though web-based training makes the information accessible to learners 24/7, it should be strongly encouraged that employees use work time for this level of professional development.

7. **Define in advance what success will look like.** Keep in mind, online training is not for everyone. The most successful organizations that implement web-based training have about a 30% participation rate. And that's fine taking into consideration that still 40% of learners would prefer in-classroom training the first time they are learning something new, and another 30% could go either way. However, for recurrent training the overwhelming majority of learners are pleased with online learning as an alternative because it saves time.

8. **Regularly measure success.** Send out brief surveys to participants in the program to ensure it is meeting their expectations and impacting key business priorities. Your survey should not only ask how participants felt about the online workshops, but also how has it helped them improve productivity, and what have they applied. Organizations who successfully implement web-based training programs not only measure participant reaction to the workshops, but also their ability to change behaviors and impact business results.

9. **Link the program to business objectives.** Like many others, your organizational goals most likely include increasing: *growth and expansion, bottom-line profit, customer satisfaction, employee engagement, and product or service quality*. Integrating online training that will contribute to these key business priorities is vital to its success. Online training topics that focus on *business and financial acumen, employee coaching and counseling, attracting and retaining top talent, workplace harassment prevention,*

diversity awareness, and *strategic planning*, all contribute to achieving common business objectives.

10. **Keep senior leadership involved and abreast.** Periodically communicate results of the online program to senior leaders. Solicit their advice on how to improve the program, topics they would like to see covered, and their involvement as subject matter experts. Anything that can be done to get them onboard as champions of the web-based training initiative should be considered, because if they believe in the program and visualize success, it will be sustainable for years to come.

In the final analysis, web-based training is a great component to add to any learning and development strategy because it not only can help reduce training time and cost, but also increase the accessibility of learning and development programs, and enhance the skill and knowledge of your staff.

SUMMARY QUESTIONS

- What topics would you like to see offered to your team in the form of web-based training?

- What is your experience with web-based training?

- How could you make it work within your organization?

Chapter 27

Employee Training & Development during Lean Times – The 5 Essentials

During lean economic times, all employee learning and development should *not* be eliminated. There are five *core learning and development essentials* that should be hastened to ensure your organization can weather the financial storm, retain its customer-based, and enhance customer loyalty.

1. **Customer Service Training** – when budget dollars and staffing are reduced, customer service diminishes if the remaining employees are not constantly reminded of just how important maintaining high levels of customer service are to the long-term viability of the organization. If classroom training is out of the question, consider informal training like E-learning or open discussions during monthly departmental meetings to reinforce the key issues. At a minimum, customer service basics that should be covered include: the proper greeting of a customer; working with a sense of urgency; telephone, voicemail, and email etiquette; and effective customer problem resolution.

2. **Cross-Training** – during lean times your staff should be multi-dimensional, enabling them to perform several different departmental job functions with skill and confidence. Tough economic times often present the greatest opportunity for job enlargement and career advancement because managers have no alternative but to make time

to train staff members to effectively multi-task. An example might be that employees who generally work in frontline positions could also be cross-trained to handle some of the routine administrative or back office tasks like *ordering basic supplies, running departmental reports, data-entry, answering and directing incoming calls* – so that during downtime they are still productive. The ultimate value of cross-training is that it opens the door to quality improvement because a new set of eyes learning how work gets done in other departments always raises awareness of how to perform the task more effectively and efficiently.

3. **Budgeting & Forecasting** – during lean times the way the departmental budgets and forecasting of sales and revenue are formulated may be different than under normal circumstances. Therefore, all leaders should be retrained *(by the appropriate senior leaders in accounting and finance)* on any updated processes to maximize financial results. Through this exercise, you'll be amazed at the number of managers who simply don't understand the fundamental principles of budgeting and forecasting, or how it relates to the work they do. Even non-revenue producing department leaders should be required to attend this session.

4. **Workplace Safety** – lean times are not a logical reason to scale back on safety issues within the workplace. Staff members often get so caught up in the frenzy of doing more with less that they sometimes create unsafe shortcuts in work practices that down the road could lead to serious injury, lawsuits, or worst the fatality of an employee or customer. Safety in the workplace can never be over-emphasized.

5. **Technology Training** – often we find that the current technology in place has several efficiency features that are not being used because no one had time to learn them in the past. Well, this is a great time to get your technology reps back out to your site for some recurrent staff training. There may be reports or other administrative processes being done manually, that could more efficiently be facilitated through

computer software you already have. When employees are properly taught to use all of the amenities and features your computer technology has to offer, it opens up more time for them to spend in front of the customer.

In the final analysis, fine tuning *(not eliminating)* employee training and development during lean economic times will ensure your organization maintains a highly skilled and empowered workforce, flexible enough to shift gears when needed to maximize customer service, productivity, and ultimately bottom-line results.

Summary Questions

- *When you are operating with a limited budget, what types of training are imperative to the business and should not be eliminated?*

- *If training is totally eliminated during tough economic times, what impact (positive and negative) would it have on the operation?*

Conclusion

My hope is that you have benefited from reading this book. My intent is to show you that effective leaders work on themselves first, then slowly through their actions and behaviors co-workers, colleagues, and others come onboard.

Don't stop here, I urge you to share the knowledge you have gained with others and commit to applying something that you have learned every day.

Acknowledgement

I would like to especially thank my family members, friends and colleagues who encourage, support, and bring purpose to my work every day.

I am also appreciative of the many clients and business leaders who engage me in deeper discussions that lead me to challenge conventional thinking.

Most of all, I thank God for the opportunity to share my thoughts and insights with the world. Without Him, I would not have the inspiration to write books that enrich the lives of others. May God abundantly bless you in your endeavor toward excellence.

Theo Gilbert-Jamison
Chief Executive Officer
Performance Solutions by Design, Inc.

About the Author

THEO GILBERT-JAMISON is the author of the popular leadership books, The Six Principles of Service Excellence, and The Leadership Book of Numbers Volume 1. She is also Chief Executive Officer of Performance Solutions by Design, an elite performance consulting firm that caters to luxury and premium brands with an emphasis on creating the ultimate customer experience.

As the creative force behind the innovative concepts and methodologies utilized by Performance Solutions by Design, Theo is a highly sought after speaker and consultant to senior executives in high profile organizations. Under her leadership, Performance Solutions by Design assists organizations, great and small, in driving and sustaining a culture of service, performance, and operational excellence by helping them identify and overcome barriers that encumber achieving world-class recognition in customer service and profitability.

Prior to launching Performance Solutions by Design in 2003, Theo Gilbert-Jamison was Vice President of Training & Organizational Effectiveness for the Ritz-Carlton Hotel Company, L.L.C. During a 17-year career with The Ritz-Carlton, she oversaw the daily operations of The Ritz-Carlton Leadership Center and was also responsible for the company's worldwide training and development initiatives.

Today, Theo works closely with a diverse group of organizations, ranging from automotive, legal and financial services, to technology, education, hospitality, healthcare, country clubs, and luxury retail. Theo is currently working on her forth book, Becoming a Level Three Organization, scheduled to be published soon.

Other Books by Theo Gilbert-Jamison

The Six Principles of Service Excellence *(2005)*

The Six Principles Workbook *(2006)*

The Organizational Alignment Library *(2006)*

The Leadership Book of Numbers, Volume 1 *(2008)*

The Leadership Book of Numbers, Volume 2 *(2012)*

Becoming a Level Three Organization *(coming soon)*

Website
www.psbydesign.com

INDEX

A

Accountability 10, 16, 27, 40, 43, 46, 47, 48, 49, 50, 52, 68, 73, 77, 79, 81, 83, 104, 105, 107
Alignment 19, 26, 45, 67, 71, 116

B

Bad Boss 39, 40, 41
Business Acumen 50, 51, 52, 68
Business Objectives 10, 11, 17, 21, 22, 23, 25, 44, 51, 80, 108, 109

C

Career 44, 59, 66, 78, 92, 95, 98, 99, 100, 110, 115
C-Level 3, 94, 95
Coach 21, 41, 48, 64, 100
Communication 4, 5, 24, 25, 33, 34, 35, 39, 44, 45, 50, 51, 52, 59, 76, 82, 86, 87, 91, 94
Conflict 63, 78, 79
Cost of Non-Compliance 14, 15
Cross-Training 78, 86, 87, 110, 111
Culture v, 3, 5, 7, 9, 10, 11, 12, 31, 33, 35, 47, 49, 71, 77, 79, 83, 97, 115
Customer Experience 3, 4, 10, 11, 14, 15, 16, 22, 115
Customer Loyalty 16, 33, 46, 70, 71, 86, 94, 95, 110

D

Delegation 67, 68, 70

E

Effectiveness iii, v, 17, 22, 37, 39, 41, 43, 45, 52, 53, 54, 57, 62, 63, 66, 68, 70, 96, 107, 115
E-Learning 110

Employee Engagement 33, 35, 36, 70, 77, 93, 108
Employee Involvement 4
Empower 68, 70
Empowerment 4, 24, 40, 45, 67, 68, 70, 77, 104
Expectations 4, 5, 9, 11, 12, 31, 36, 39, 43, 45, 46, 47, 49, 53, 108

F

Feedback 4, 18, 34, 44, 53, 57, 76, 78, 94, 103
Follow-Up 4, 5, 24, 28, 74, 83, 92, 105

G

Goals 5, 23, 39, 40, 43, 51, 70, 83, 94, 103, 108

H

HR Standards 91, 93

I

Implement 12, 77, 82, 98, 100, 101, 105, 108
Improve 20, 32, 41, 49, 52, 57, 58, 66, 68, 76, 79, 85, 95, 103, 108, 109
Improvement 11, 34, 40, 43, 49, 57, 65, 77, 79, 80, 111
Inefficiencies 69, 77, 80, 85, 87
Innovation 7, 43, 50, 51, 52, 78
Input 4, 8, 18, 19, 68, 76, 94, 103
Internal Customers 3, 26, 28, 29
Interviewing 11, 71, 97
Involvement 4, 7, 8, 9, 34, 73, 94, 95, 104, 109

K

Key Touch Points 4, 11, 30, 31

L

Lean Staff 76, 77, 78, 79
Learning & Development iii, v, 89, 91
Low Performers 81

M

Measurement 31, 48
Memorable Experience 86
Mid-Managers 8, 9, 10, 11, 16, 18, 81
Mission 23
Mystery Shopping 30

N

Network 99

P

Pilot 95
Powerful Presentations 53
Priorities 10, 21, 22, 23, 44, 51, 52, 67, 69, 94, 108
Problem Resolution 24
Process 3, 4, 8, 11, 16, 24, 30, 31, 32, 34, 40, 46, 48, 49, 55, 71, 72, 73, 74, 75, 77, 78, 80, 81, 85, 92, 100, 104, 105, 111
Professional Presence 59, 62
Project Owner 4
Purpose iv, v, 18, 21, 22, 23, 26, 30, 31, 32, 65, 67, 107, 114

Q

Quantify 48, 95

R

Raise the Bar 47, 71
Recessionary Times 85
Recognition 4, 25, 35, 83, 93, 115
Recruitment 71, 97, 98, 99, 100, 101
Refine 19, 58, 80, 95
Respect 23, 27, 28, 29, 44, 57, 61, 63, 78, 92
Results 16, 24, 33, 34, 43, 45, 46, 48, 49, 51, 53, 76, 79, 87, 98, 108, 109, 111, 112
Retain 75, 81, 83, 97, 98, 101, 102, 104, 105, 110
Retool 82
Reward 4, 12, 24, 25, 31, 35, 44, 48, 52, 77, 83, 93, 106, 107
Ritz-Carlton 22, 47, 91, 94, 99, 115

S

Selection 31, 71, 72, 73, 74, 75, 92, 97, 100, 101, 107
Senior Leadership 3, 5, 6, 7, 8, 9, 10, 12, 18, 20, 21, 43, 50, 65, 96, 109
Service Excellence iii, v, 1, 3, 5, 6, 9, 17, 24, 25, 26, 27, 28, 29, 47, 54, 91, 115, 116
Service Philosophy 22, 43
Solution 4, 8, 24, 48, 65, 114, 115
Standards 4, 18, 25, 28, 39, 40, 43, 44, 45, 59, 73, 91, 93
Strategy 11, 14, 16, 20, 40, 48, 50, 51, 52, 80, 82, 83, 86, 87, 94, 95, 100, 101, 109
Streamline 77, 80

T

Talent 72
Teamwork 23, 27, 44, 48, 77, 92
Technology 14, 15, 55, 68, 72, 111, 112, 115
Time Management 67, 68, 69, 70
Tools & Resources 34
Training 3, 4, 11, 14, 24, 26, 31, 40, 45, 48, 54, 55, 57, 69, 70, 78, 82, 83, 86, 87, 91, 92, 93, 96, 98, 99, 103, 104, 105, 106, 108, 109, 110, 111, 112, 115
Trust 23, 33, 34, 35, 70, 76, 77

U

Unacceptable Behavior 12, 63, 65, 66

V

Vision 4, 7, 9, 10, 11, 17, 18, 19, 20, 21, 22, 23, 25, 98

W

Warm Body 101
Web-based Training 83, 106, 107, 108, 109
Work Environment 4, 5, 10, 11, 12, 19, 22, 23, 24, 25, 34, 35, 39, 41, 43, 45, 48, 52, 60, 63, 66, 73, 76, 77, 79, 91, 92, 93, 97, 98, 101, 103, 106

www.ingramcontent.com/pod-product-compliance
Lightning Source LLC
Chambersburg PA
CBHW030816180526
45163CB00003B/1310